"ASTONISHING."
The Seattle Times

"CLOSER TO THE LIGHT is a quick and compelling read. It is upbeat and heartening, especially to those who have survived the death of a loved one."

Trenton Times

"Daring . . . An amazing book."

Fairfax Journal (VA)

"Terrific reading."

The Union Leader (Manchester, NH)

"Highly readable."

Booklist

CLOSER TO THE LIGHT

Learning from the Near-Death
Experiences of Children

Melvin Morse, M.D., with Paul Perry

IVY BOOKS • NEW YORK

Ivy Books
Published by Ballantine Books
Copyright © 1990 by Dr. Melvin L. Morse and Paul Perry

Grateful acknowledgment is made to the following for permission to reprint previously published material: PANTHEON BOOKS: An excerpt from *Memories, Dreams, Reflections* by Carl G. Jung, recorded and edited by Aniela Jaffe, translated by Richard and Clara Winston. Translation copyright © 1961, 1962, 1963 by Random House, Inc. Reprinted by permission of Pantheon Books, a division of Random House, Inc. PRINCETON UNIVERSITY PRESS: Excerpts from *Mystery of the Mind* by Wilder Penfield. Copyright © 1975 by Princeton University Press. Reprinted by permission of Princeton University Press.

Library of Congress Catalog Card Number: 90-31841

ISBN 0-8041-0832-3

This edition published by arrangement with Villard Books, a division of Random House, Inc.

Manufactured in the United States of America

First Ballantine Books Edition: September 1991

To my wife Allison
and children,
Bridget, Colleen and Brett,
for their patience and inspiration.
                              —Melvin Morse, M.D.

For my mother, Esther,
and my father, Jewel.

                              —Paul Perry

ABOUT THE CASE STUDIES

The case studies in this book represent material gathered during interviews with patients who had near-death experiences.

Names, ages and some of the details of these stories have been changed to protect the identity of the patients.

Foreword

With the publication of *Life After Life* more than a decade ago, I issued a challenge to the people in the medical profession to continue researching the marvelous phenomenon of the near-death experience.

Many physicians and researchers accepted that challenge. They began looking at this amazing spiritual experience in a variety of ways with the multitude of tools and methods available in medicine. Their work has spawned a vast new area of research known as near-death studies.

Of all the researchers to enter this brave new world of spiritual studies, the most interesting and arresting work has been done by Melvin Morse.

Dr. Morse is a compassionate pediatrician who was introduced to the near-death experience through the near drowning of one of his young patients, a shy and lovely girl named Katie. She had hovered on the brink of death for three days. She was in such a deep coma that machines were required to keep her breathing. No one, including Dr. Morse, expected her to live.

At the end of the third day, she simply awoke as if she had been in a deep sleep. Within twenty-four hours, this sleeping beauty was up and around, talking to her family, and showing no signs of brain damage.

It was a miracle indeed, but it wasn't until a few days after she awoke that Dr. Morse discovered the real miracle. He was curious to know what had caused her accident. Had someone pushed her underwater? Had a seizure caused her to lose consciousness while swimming? These are the usual kinds of questions asked by physicians so they can provide adequate treatment. The answers Dr. Morse received were really quite unusual.

When he asked her what happened in the pool, Katie said, "You mean when I saw the Heavenly Father?" She then went on to describe this marvelous spiritual journey through "heaven" that left Dr. Morse spellbound. She told him of seeing "God," a man of bright light who filled her with his love and kindness. She told of being guided by a guardian angel named Elizabeth who showed her heaven and even let her return home once to see her family. She then told of God's offer to let her stay or return to her mother. She chose to return, she said, which was why she was here now.

Katie's story stayed with Dr. Morse. Rather than dismiss it as a dream or as an example of "a few wires getting crossed," he decided to undertake some research projects that would look at this phenomenon scientifically. With the help of a major hospital in Seattle, Dr. Morse was able to pick up where I had left off in answering humanity's most nagging question: What happens when we die?

Here are just some of the marvelous discoveries of Dr. Morse and his research team:

- They have proven that a person actually needs to be near death to *have* a near-death experience. This finding silenced many skeptics who had said that these events were just hallucinations that any seriously ill patient could have. By scientifically comparing the experiences of seriously ill patients with those who had been on the brink of death, the team was able to determine that one does need to cross that threshold before glimpsing the other side.
- They have been able to isolate the area in the brain where near-death experiences occur. This area, close to the right temporal lobe, is genetically coded for near-death experiences. Dr. Morse and his researchers explored whether this could be the "seat of the soul," the area that holds the vital essence that makes us what we are.

Dr. Morse has also drawn on the works of the world's great neuroscientists to support his belief that the same "something" that makes us live (many of us call it the "soul") survives bodily death. As you'll see in reading this book, even such hard-core scientists as brain surgeons have grappled with that amorphous issue of the human soul.

Dr. Morse's book is filled with the courage it takes

to act with compassion. For instance, where other doctors reject predeath visions as being caused by fever or fear, Dr. Morse accepts them as help for the dying and uses them to create a soothing environment for patients. From this compassion has risen some intriguing psychic phenomena. As you'll see, there are many cases in which children who are near death have been able to summon distant relatives to their bedside. Some of these children have even been able to communicate with dead friends and relatives, reporting things that they could never have known without actual contact with the dead.

Most doctors have been trained to use tranquilizers, not their ears, to deal with the visions of the dying. It takes courage to go against training. Yet in doing so, Dr. Morse has made some startling discoveries that could easily redefine the way the dying are dealt with.

In his quest to look at all aspects of the near-death experience, Dr. Morse has painstakingly tracked down adults who had almost died as children. His goal was to examine the long-term effects of these experiences, to see if they gave life new meaning. After listening to dozens of stories (many of which you will read here), Dr. Morse discovered that these "experiences of light" brighten a person's life forever.

As a physician, it takes wisdom to listen and learn and admit that everything about the human body and mind can't be taught in medical school. Dr. Morse has bravely stepped out of traditional parameters to take a scientific look at near-death experiences, psychic phenomena, and the existence of the soul.

His explorations have paid off for him in a rewarding life and for us in an intriguing and useful book.

—Raymond A. Moody, M.D.

ACKNOWLEDGMENTS

This book could only have been possible with the co-operation and trust of hundreds of patients who have shared their experiences with me. In some cases I have changed minor details and edited experiences so as to protect the identities of those involved.

Archie Bleyer, M.D., was a constant source of insight and inspiration. I am deeply indebted to him for the years I spent learning from him as his research fellow. Those years were truly the golden years and he helped me to make the most productive use of them. Donald Tyler, M.D., helped me with his open mind and thoughtful comments on research design. Mark Smith, M.D., provided me with invaluable emotional support. Jerrold Milstein, M.D., was my adviser. Most of the work on the anatomical location of near-death experiences is his contribution. John Neff, M.D., supplied me with an often-needed shoulder to cry on and much needed sage advice.

Paula Livesly typed all my original manuscripts and gently nagged me to complete my deadlines. Tanya S. provided essential secretarial assistance as well as many thoughtful insights into our research design and interviewing techniques.

My own office staff has helped me above and beyond the call of duty. I am particularly indebted to Penny Kellog, Tiki Hunnicutt, and Nancy Henry for handling the thousands of details and messages on tiny pieces of paper that I would otherwise have lost track of.

Raymond Moody, M.D., and Bruce Greyson, M.D., are my mentors in near-death research, and whatever I have contributed is only because of what they have already achieved. My agent Nat Sobel is the soul of this book and brought me together with Paul Perry, the writer, and Diane Reverand, my editor at Random House. Nat also taught me how to write a book and to believe in myself. Diane Reverand sculpted the manuscript into its current form, and believe me, it is vastly improved over my original version.

I particularly am grateful for the support of my partners Margaret Clements and David Christopher. In the three years that I have labored over this book they have been patient with me in a thousand different ways. I would never have been able to find time to write this book without their support.

Finally, I thank my mother, for everything.

1

Katie Meets Elizabeth

Let the little children be, and do not hinder them from coming to me, for such is the Kingdom of Heaven.
—*Matthew 19:14*

I stood over Katie's lifeless body in the intensive care unit and wondered whether this little girl could be saved. A few hours earlier she had been found floating facedown in a YMCA pool. No one knew how long she had been unconscious or exactly what had happened to cause her to lose consciousness. One of the lifeguards guessed that some boys playing alongside the pool had accidentally knocked her into the water. Someone else mentioned to the police that maybe she had bumped her head on the bottom of the pool and had lost consciousness that way. It could even have been an epileptic seizure, I thought.

I didn't really expect to find out what had happened. The machines to which she was now hooked up told a grim story. An emergency CAT scan showed massive swelling of the brain. She had no gag reflex. An artificial lung machine was breathing for her. In the blunt jargon of emergency room physicians, she was a train wreck. Looking back even now, I would guess that she had only a ten percent chance of surviving.

I was the doctor who resuscitated her in the emergency room after the accident in the pool. I was serving my internship in pediatrics in a small town in Idaho and would be starting my residency a few months later in Seattle. I had previously been doing research on brain tumors and at a national conference had presented a paper on the effects of chemotherapy on childhood leukemia. In between the world of academia studies and "rat brain" research, in which I tested the effects of various medicines on white rats, I wanted to sandwich in some practical medicine. Medicine probably doesn't get more practical than poor Katie's case.

She was one of the sickest children I have ever cared for. Despite all of our best efforts, I was sure she was going to die. Still we tried everything we could think of.

THE CIRCLE OF PRAYER

One episode with Katie remains vivid in my mind even today. I was trying to thread a small catheter into one of her arteries so we could get an exact reading of the oxygen in her blood. The procedure, called arterial catheterization, is particularly difficult and bloody since an incision into an artery is required.

I explained the procedure to her father and told him that he and the other family members might want to wait in the hall until the line was inserted. He consulted with his wife and the others and came back with another suggestion. He asked if they could hold a prayer vigil around her bed while I threaded the device into her artery. Why not? I thought. She's going to die anyway. Maybe this will help them cope with their grief.

The family held hands around her bed and began to pray. Katie lay flat and lifeless as breathing machines and monitors beeped and buzzed and several IV tubes gave her fluids and medication. Two nurses and a respiratory therapist were with me. One push of the needle and blood began spurting from the arterial line. We all did our jobs quickly and nervously. It seems now that the calmest people in the room were the members of Katie's family. As the blood spurted out, they began praying out loud.

How can they be so calm? I thought. Isn't it obvious that she is going to die?

Three days later she made a full recovery.

Her case was one of those medical mysteries that demonstrate the power of the human organism to rebound. People sometimes cross the threshold of death only to return in full health. Why it happens is impossible to say. But it happened with Katie, whose neurological testing showed she had made a full recovery.

When she was feeling well enough, I had her come in for a follow-up examination. One of the things I wanted to know was what she remembered about her near drowning. The answer was important to the type of treatment she would receive as an outpatient. Had she been hit on the head? Had someone held her under the water? Had she blacked out or experienced a seizure? Without knowing exactly what had happened, there was a chance that she could have another blackout or seizure.

I marveled at Katie when she came into the office. She was a pretty girl with long blond hair and a shy, frightened manner. Her eyes revealed an intelligence that hadn't been dimmed by the deprivation of oxygen to the brain that always accompanies drowning. There was nothing abnormal in her walk or mannerisms. She was just another nine-year-old kid.

THE HEAVENLY FATHER

Katie clearly remembered me. After introducing myself, she turned to her mother and said, "That's the one with the beard. First there was this tall doctor who didn't have a beard, and then he came in." Her statement was correct. The first into the emergency room was a tall, clean-shaven physician named Bill Longhurst.

Katie remembered more. "First I was in the big room, and then they moved me to a smaller room where they did X-rays on me." She accurately noted such details as having "a tube down my nose," which was her description of nasal intubation. Most physicians intubate orally, and that is the most common way that it is represented on television.

She accurately described many other details of her experience. I remember being amazed at the events she recollected. Even though her eyes had been closed and she had been profoundly comatose during the entire experience, she still "saw" what was going on.

I asked her an open-ended question: "What do you remember about being in the swimming pool?"

"Do you mean when I visited the Heavenly Father," she replied.

Whoa, I thought. "That's a good place to start. Tell me about meeting the Heavenly Father."

"I met Jesus and the Heavenly Father," she said. Maybe it was the shocked look on my face or maybe it was shyness. But that was it for the day. She became very embarrassed and would speak no more.

I scheduled her for another appointment the following week.

What she told me during our next meeting changed my life. She remembered nothing about the drowning itself. Her first memory was of darkness and the feeling that she was so heavy she couldn't move. Then a tunnel opened and through that tunnel came "Elizabeth."

Elizabeth was "tall and nice" with bright, golden hair. She accompanied Katie up the tunnel, where she saw her late grandfather and met several other people. Among her "new friends" were two young boys—"souls waiting to be born"—named Andy and Mark, who played with her and introduced her to many people.

At one point in the voyage, Katie was given a glimpse of her home. She was allowed to wander throughout the house, watching her brothers and sisters play with their toys in their rooms. One of her brothers was playing with a GI Joe, pushing him around the room in a jeep. One of her sisters was combing the hair of a Barbie doll and singing a popular rock song. She drifted into the kitchen and watched her mother preparing a meal of roast chicken and rice. Then she looked into the living room and saw her father sitting on the couch staring quietly ahead. She assumed he was worrying about her in the hospital.

Later, when Katie mentioned this to her parents, she shocked them with her vivid details about the clothing they were wearing, their positions in the house, even the food her mother was cooking.

Finally, Elizabeth—who seemed to be a guardian angel to Katie—took her to meet the Heavenly Father and Jesus. The Heavenly Father asked if she wanted to go home. Katie cried. She said she wanted to stay with him. Then Jesus asked her if she wanted to see her mother again. "Yes," she replied. Then she awoke.

It took her almost an hour to tell this story. She was extremely shy, but told the tale in such a powerful and compelling way that I believed her implicitly. Throughout the telling of her experience, she drew pictures of the people she had met while in "heaven."

Elizabeth was drawn as a pleasant, smiling stick figure with white clothing. Mark and Andy looked like drawings of ordinary schoolmates. Clearly, this had been a fun event for a child so young. She didn't yet have a concept of religious or mystical experience. She was aware that something had happened that she didn't quite understand.

I didn't understand it either. I began to investigate.

First I went to the nurses in the intensive care unit, who told me that the first words out of her mouth when she awoke were "Where are Mark and Andy?" She asked for them repeatedly throughout her convalescence.

Then I probed her family's religious beliefs. I wanted to see if she had been heavily indoctrinated with belief in guardian angels and tunnels to heaven.

The answer from her mother was an emphatic no. She was a middle-of-the-road Mormon. She believed in the afterlife and attended Sunday school regularly, but no one in the family espoused a belief in spirit guides or tunnels to heaven. These things simply never came up in the family's religious teachings. In fact, I could find little similarity between Katie's experience and any of her religious teachings.

For instance, two years before Katie's experience, when her grandfather had died, Katie had been told by her mother that death was like sending someone on a long boat ride: friends and family can go to the edge of the water, but they must stay on land while the boat floats away. Her mother had described the soul as "the hand in the glove." When a glove has a hand in it, it is alive and moving. After the hand is removed, the glove looks the same but doesn't move.

No one in the family had mentioned anything that would trigger the images that came to Katie at the brink of death.

My curiosity grew. I recounted the experience for Dr. Chris Robison, a chief resident at the hospital and also a devout Mormon. From him, I learned that Mormons believe in Christ and an afterlife, but not in spirit guides and guardian angels. They also have no scriptural reason to believe that heaven is a place you get to by going through a tunnel.

I spent hours talking with her parents, trying to discover any factors in her upbringing that could have influenced her experience. I couldn't find any.

My deepest instinct told me that nothing in Katie's experience was "taught" to her before the near drowning. Her experience was fresh, not recalled memory.

I began looking through the medical literature.

A NEAR-DEATH EXPERIENCE

A search of the medical literature revealed little besides a name for what had happened to Katie. It was called "the near-death experience" (NDE).

The name for this phenomenon was coined by Dr. Raymond Moody in his 1975 book, *Life After Life*. Near-death experience, or NDE, is used to describe a mystical experience that happens to people who almost die.

A poll conducted by the George Gallup organization found in an extensive survey an estimated eight million near-death experiences in 1982. Needless to say, these are very controversial events. Some say that NDEs are just dramas created by the mind in a state of panic. Others say that they are glimpses into the next world.

Researchers such as Raymond Moody and Kenneth Ring assume that only those who cross death's door have vivid trips up tunnels or see long-dead relatives and Beings of Light. Other researchers, including psychologist Ron Siegel, believe that NDEs are visions brought on by drugs or "dissociative hallucinatory activity of the brain."

What we now know as near-death experiences have been reported since the beginning of recorded history. In the New Testament (2 Cor. 12:1–4), Paul describes one that he had. And Pope Gregory the Great in the sixth century collected these experiences as proof of life beyond.

Carol Zaleski, a prominent Harvard theologian, finds near-death experiences in Greek, Roman, Egyptian, and Near Eastern myths and legends. I was fascinated to read in her book, *Otherworld Journeys*, that some cultures see death as a journey whose final goal is the recovery of one's true nature.

It wasn't until 1975, when Dr. Raymond Moody published his findings, that anyone realized there was a pattern to the experiences. Something mystical and unearthly happened to many people who had almost died.

According to Moody, a full-blown near-death experience happens something like this: A person, say, has a heart attack in his living room. The chest pain is excruciating, and he passes out. What seems like moments later, he awakens to find himself floating above his body, where he watches the paramedics administering CPR. He tries to stop them, but it becomes obvious that they can't hear him.

Suddenly, a tunnel appears to this disembodied spirit. He finds himself zooming up it with the whooshing sound of speed in his ears. His trip ends in a garden of rich green plants, one that is glowing with unearthly light. He looks at his own hands and realizes that he too is composed of light.

People approach him. They are glowing too. Some of them look familiar. There's Uncle George, who died twenty years ago. And Aunt Mabel. Even Grandfather is here in radiant glory. All of them are happy to see this visitor, feelings they are able to express nonverbally with their warmth.

These glowing personages pale in comparison to what comes next. A master Being of Light appears. Some call him "God," others "Allah," and others "The Man." Whoever he is, he is so bright and loving that the visitor feels drawn to him.

With more love and caring than this visitor had ever felt from anyone on earth, the master Being of Light engulfs him with his presence, taking him on a three-dimensional review of his life. Not only does he see everything he has done to anybody, but he feels everything as well. In addition to experiencing the way he felt when it happened, the visitor knows how it felt to the other person. This sensory barrage is accompanied by a moral commentary from the Being of Light, who compassionately communicates to the person what he did right and wrong and indicates things he might do in the future.

The problem is that the person wants this experience to go on forever. He doesn't want to leave the Being of Light's bosom. He tells this to the being, but is given no choice. He must return.

Suddenly, he feels himself sucked back into his own body, where he becomes a changed person. The type-A behavior that made him an edgy, angry workaholic is now gone.

Replacing these traits is a thirst for knowledge, feelings, and expressions of love that astonishes the people who know him.

COLLECTOR OF TALES

Moody first learned about NDEs when he was twenty years old and studying for his doctorate in philosophy at the University of Virginia. While studying philosophical issues related to death, his professor told him about a psychiatrist in town who had been pronounced dead of double pneumonia and then successfully resuscitated. While he was "dead," the doctor later said, he'd had the remarkable experience of passing through a tunnel and seeing Beings of Light. Moody filed the story away in his memory and went on with his studies. In 1969, he finished his doctorate and began teaching at his alma mater. After conducting a class dealing with the afterlife, Moody was approached by a student who had almost died in an automobile accident the year before. The student told Moody a baffling tale that almost mirrored the psychiatrist's experience he had heard when he was a student.

Moody told the two stories to his students. They, in turn, shared tales of aunts, uncles, grandparents, and friends who'd had similar experiences during their brushes with death. By the time he entered medical school, in 1972, Moody had compiled eight case studies from people he describes as "solid and reliable."

In medical school, he was able to find more cases. It soon became clear to him that near-death experiences were much more common than he had expected. "In any group of thirty," says Moody, "I can find someone who has had one or knows someone who has had one."

TRADITIONAL VIEW QUESTIONED

Katie intrigued me. The more time I spent with her, the more I questioned the traditional medical approach to this issue. Basically, medicine didn't acknowledge the existence of these experiences. Although something had happened to one of my patients—something so real that it was having lasting, positive effects upon her—I could find scant mention of the near-death experience in medical journals. I had to turn to Moody's book, which was outside the medical mainstream, to find out what had happened to my patient.

After my experience with Katie, I decided to do something no other medical doctor had done. I published a description of Katie's NDE in a medical journal. To my knowledge, this was the first description of a near-death experience in a child. I wanted other pediatricians to know that children had such experiences. My main motivation was to get doctors to contemplate the meaning of these experiences so they could help patients understand the dying process. I thought nothing could be more universal than the psychological events of dying.

In 1983 my article was published in the *American Journal of Diseases of Children*. I almost stopped my inquiry there. Then I remembered what Moody had said in his second book, *Reflections on Life After Life*. He wrote that if anyone were to research the topic with an open mind he would be convinced of the reality of near-death experiences. He recognized that his work was not scientific, but was merely an examination of a collection of personal anecdotes.

It was then that I decided to do more than write one article. I felt challenged by Dr. Moody's bold assertions, especially by his claim that these experiences were universal to all human beings.

Many questions began to pop into my mind:

- *Do children have NDEs that are different from those of adults*? Since children aren't yet "culturally polluted," some people claim that they don't have near-death experiences or that those they do have are very different. Katie's NDE was similar to those of adults. But what about other children?

As a professor of mine at George Washington University said, "Children don't lie." Of course they lie about doing their homework or cleaning their rooms. By this she meant that in the context of a severe illness they would probably not fabricate such stories. In addition, they would most likely not have heard about the phenomenon of the near-death experience. Studying children would give me an opportunity to deal with a pure population.

I could find no research similar to this in the medical journals.

- *Does one need to be near death to have an NDE?* Some people say that these are merely hallucinations of a frightened mind and can occur to people who aren't near death. Others have assumed that NDEs can be caused by the drugs we give patients or even by their profound fear of the intensive care unit. I found myself wanting to know the answer to this question. I designed a study to unravel the puzzle because I found no study remotely resembling this in the medical literature.
- *Is there an area of the brain that produces near-death experiences?* This was the most exciting question of all. Dr. Moody asserts that these experiences happen in all human beings. If so, perhaps there is an area of the brain that is genetically programmed to create these experiences.

  Why would such an area be there? We could only attempt to answer that question. Finding it would have exciting implications for understanding the experience.
- *Have the researchers missed any traits?* Is there anything else that happens during a near-death experi-

ence that the researchers didn't discover? My
positions on the staffs of two major hospitals would
give me access to raw data. I could talk with patients
right after NDEs happened.
- *How did NDEs affect children after they became
  adults*? NDEs are known to be transformative experiences that greatly change attitudes in the people
  who have them. I wanted to know if children who
  have them are changed throughout their lives?

No research existed to answer that question.

BLUNTING FEAR OF FAILURE

In treating Katie, I discovered a significant gap in the
medical literature. I also discovered another, more
disturbing gap. Although death and dying are now the
province of the physician, most aren't comfortable
with the subject. They regard death as a sign of personal failure, final confirmation of the limitations of
medicine. Many of us use our professional knowledge
as a buffer against death, a way to blunt our own anxieties.

It should have come as no surprise when Katie's
experience was greeted with some skepticism and
doubt by my colleagues. Most of the doctors I talked
to thought her experience was a freak hallucination
that I embellished. Some of my friends implied that I
was probably hallucinating as well and took to whis-
tling the theme to *The Twilight Zone* whenever I would
bring up the subject.

Many of my medical colleagues thought that near-death experiences shouldn't be dignified by scientific investigation. Quite frankly, many of them felt that the subject had received too much exposure in supermarket tabloids to be taken seriously by medical science. Anything reported in tabloid newspapers that ran such articles as "I Dated Bigfoot" could not be taken seriously, they reasoned.

I feel that medical science has tried to sweep the near-death experience under the carpet for other reasons. I think it raises the question of whether there is life after death, a question that defies the rigid objectivity hammered into us in medical school. It is easy to dismiss NDEs as "supernatural" or to put them into the same category as UFO sightings.

The physicians' attitudes on near-death experiences must have been apparent to their patients. Although I spoke to psychiatrists and psychologists about Katie's NDE, few of them had ever heard an experience being described by a patient.

Even the head of psychiatry was skeptical. He had a nationwide reputation from his work on death and dying. He helped me search the literature and to structure studies I was considering. But still he was doubtful.

"Mel, Katie's experience is a complete fascinoma," he declared one day in his office after reading her case study. "A case like this has never been reported before. Children don't have near-death experiences."

The nursing staff had a different response. They told of many similar experiences occurring among their patients. Perhaps the difference was in how they treated their patients. Where the doctors were generally brusque and hurried, the nurses spent more time talking and listening.

All of this made me more curious.

Maybe I was driven by Katie's deep sincerity when she told of the miraculous journey she had taken. Maybe the driving factor was Raymond Moody's bold assertion that if someone were to conduct a scientific study it would confirm his findings that NDEs do exist. I vowed to conduct scientific studies that would shed light on these so-called spiritual journeys.

Most of all, I wanted to know *what had happened to Katie*?

2

The Seattle Study

Whether there is such a thing as communication between man and God, and whether energy can come to
the mind of man from an outside source after his death
is for each individual to decide for himself. Science
has no such answers
—Wilder Penfield, the father of neurosurgery

Several months after Katie's marvelous experience, I
left Pocatella and went to Children's Hospital in Seattle.

I had a research grant to study the effects of an
anticancer chemical called methotrexate on the brains
and spinal cords of rats, which would ultimately show
how this drug effects humans.

Still, I wanted to do more than be a rodent brain
surgeon and study the effects of a drug on animals. I
wanted to research the causes and meaning of the near-
death experience. In my off-hours, I designed a study
that would answer the most basic question: Does a

person need to be *near death* to have a near-death experience? This may seem like an odd question, but it was the one that no one had really answered.

Janet Lunceford, my grant director at the National Cancer Institute, was very supportive of my research into near-death experiences. She explained that the purpose of an open-ended grant such as the one I had been given was to design and carry out the investigation of projects that came to mind during the time of the grant. They only needed to be approved in advance by her.

I began by organizing a research team. I assembled eight researchers. Among them were Dr. Don Tyler, who was chosen for his expertise in anesthetics and their effects upon the brain. Dr. Jerrold Milstein, director of the Department of Child Neurology, University of Washington, was chosen for his knowledge of brain stem and hippocampal function. For psychiatric input, I selected Dr. Bruce Greyson, head of inpatient psychiatry at the University of Connecticut and editor of the *Journal of Near-Death Studies*. He has published more than twenty papers on the subject and is considered to be the foremost scientific authority on adult near-death experiences.

Kim Clark, a nationally known near-death researcher, was chosen for her expertise in counseling people who have had near-death experiences. She is the head of the Northwest Chapter of the International Association of Near-Death Studies (IANDS).

Clark's interest in near-death studies was sparked in

a way that was similar to mine. While a young psychologist at Harborview Hospital in Seattle, she was counseling a patient named Maria who'd had a cardiac arrest. She was preparing this patient for life outside the hospital by telling her about the psychological adjustments that many heart patients must make.

The woman wasn't interested in what Clark had to say. Instead, she wanted to talk about how she had floated around the hospital while doctors struggled to start her heart.

To prove that she had left her body, the woman insisted that there was a shoe on the ledge outside Clark's window. Clark opened the window, but could see no shoe. "It's out there," the woman insisted. Clark leaned out, but still could not see the shoe. "It's around the corner," said the woman. Courageously, Clark crawled onto the ledge of her fifth-floor window and around the corner. There sat a shoe, just as Maria had described. That event triggered an interest that has led Clark to study the near-death experience.

To research whether near death is required to have a near-death experience, we assembled two groups of children. The control group consisted of 121 children who were critically ill, but not near death. These children were on artificial lung machines, were treated with tranquilizers and narcotics, and ranged in age from three to sixteen years of age and were hospitalized in the intensive care unit at Children's Hospital. They all endured the fear and psychological stress of being in an intensive care unit.

Although these children never had life-threatening episodes, they were quite ill. For instance, one girl had been completely paralyzed for three months. She was at no time near the point of death, but she would certainly have had reason to hallucinate. Another girl had a peculiar problem in which her blood pressure would suddenly plummet, causing her to lose consciousness. Other children in the control group experienced a horrifying disease known as epiglottitis, in which the cartilage protecting the windpipe suddenly swells and prevents breathing. All of them had been bedridden for a long period of time, and most had been heavily medicated at one time or another. They had experienced the effects of narcotic drugs, the same drugs that some doctors thought had created Katie's visions. All 121 children in the control group had serious diseases, but had less than a five percent chance of dying.

The study group, on the other hand, was composed of children who had looked death in the face, kids who would probably have died or faced severe handicaps had it not been for modern medical care. There were twelve in the study group. To find that many, I had to comb ten years of hospital records and interview every survivor of a near-fatal illness. They were interviewed anywhere from a few weeks to ten years after their experience.

These twelve children represented quite a collection of diseases. All of them had cardiac arrests stemming from such accidents as near drownings and automobile wrecks and such diseases as severe kidney problems, asthma, and heart stoppages during surgery. Given today's modern care, about fifty percent of cardiac arrest victims die.

My study design was quite simple. I identified myself as being a physician who was interested in the psychological experience of being in an intensive care unit. I was careful to avoid any mention of near-death research since I didn't want to influence their responses in any way. I simply said that I wanted to learn what it was like to be very sick and that I hoped they would share the experience with me, no matter how strange it might be. The average interview lasted about two hours and followed a standard list of simple questions:

- What do you remember about being sick?
- Did you have any dreams or do you remember being unconscious?
- Tell me everything you remember about being in the hospital.
- What happened next?
- What do you think happens after we die?
- Can you describe your family's religious beliefs?
- Can you draw me a picture of your experiences in the hospital?

The questions were carefully structured to be open-ended so the children weren't coached in any way. When these questions were answered, I then asked twenty-six questions from Bruce Greyson's near-death experience questionnaire. These questions deal with the specific characteristics of the near-death experience and enabled the responses of the children to be checked against the traits of NDEs.

NEAR DEATH REQUIRED

After hundreds of hours of research and questioning, I had my answer: A person does need to be near death to experience an NDE. Of the 121 seriously ill children, not one of them had anything resembling a near-death experience.

A few had vivid dreams, the type you would expect them to have. One child had the understandable dream of monsters dressed in white coats attacking her. Another remembered hearing nurses ask for medication or gloves. Of the 121 control patients, 118 had no memory at all of their hospital stay, in spite of having survived frightening illnesses and having passed through that lifesaving torture chamber known as the intensive care unit.

I went outside the control group to interview thirty-seven children who had been treated with almost every kind of mind-altering medication known to pharmacology. These children had been given anesthetic agents, narcotics, Valium, Thorazine, Haldol, Dilantin, antidepressants, mood elevators, and painkillers. My aim was to see if drugs caused the NDEs and to find out if those skeptical doctors who doubted Katie's experience were right.

None of them had anything resembling an NDE.

Even one girl who was *helped* to hallucinate didn't have any events resembling an NDE. She was a thirteen-year-old with Guillain-Barre syndrome, an affliction that causes a total body paralysis—in her case for several months. This disease begins in the feet and slowly advances toward the head. At first, walking is impossible. Then, week by week, the afflicted person can't sit up, can't breathe, and ultimately can't move any muscles. Through all of this, the Guillain-Barre victim is completely conscious and aware of what is going on around him.

The disease is extremely painful and annoying. One itches, for instance, but is unable to scratch. This itching can go on relentlessly for hours with no relief possible. With Guillain-Barre, however, the victim is never near death.

This young patient spent months suffering from the sensory and sleep deprivation associated with a stay in an intensive care unit. The only muscles she could use were those that controlled her eyelids. Because she was flat on her back in an iron lung, she saw only the lights on the ceiling.

To relieve her agony, she was liberally treated with almost every type of pain medicine available. Her pain became so severe that the doctors prescribed hypnotherapy designed to help her "leave" her body.

Despite all of this, she had no experience resembling an NDE. She remembers being hypnotized but describes it as a vague, surreal experience. "I was drifting; I could hear music," she said. "But I always knew I was being hypnotized, and it didn't really help that much with the pain."

If near-death experiences are hallucinations, why did

this patient not have any experience remotely resembling an NDE?

The experimental group, those children who had survived cardiac arrest or who had miraculously returned from deep comas, had another story all together. Most of these children had at least one of the NDE traits—being out of their physical bodies, traveling up some sort of tunnel, seeing a light, visiting with people who describe themselves as being dead, seeing a Being of Light, having a life review, and maybe even deciding consciously to return to their bodies.

Usually, they would begin to describe their NDE with a look of puzzlement and a statement similar to that of one patient who said, "Well, I kind of remember a really funny thing that I can't exactly tell you. I was looking at myself and floating. It was dark and at the same time it was light. I was going somewhere, but I didn't exactly know where."

With further prompting, they would tell their story. Some would offer fragmentary images of a powerful experience. Others would come forth with wonderful and compelling stories, much like the one from Katie. Usually, they had not told their parents about their NDE. And none told any doctor or nurse unless it slipped out while they were semiconscious.

For example, one twelve-year-old patient I interviewed was unaware of how critically ill she had been following a cardiac arrest brought on by an attack of asthma. At the end of an hour-long interview in which we discussed every aspect of her hospitalization, from how the nurses had treated her to what the food had tasted like, I closed my interview by asking, "Is there anything else that you remember about being sick?"

She wrinkled her nose and said, "Well, yes, one other thing happened, but it's hard to describe. You'll probably think I'm crazy, but I did think that I was out of my body. I thought I was looking down at myself. I could see my mother holding my hand, and I could see a light."

All of the children were puzzled by what had occurred. They knew something special had happened, but their youth made them unsure of just what it was. For some, the experience meant nothing special. It happened and that was that. For others, it led to profound changes. Some of these children feel they were brought back for a purpose. Some are more mature than their friends or are now better students. None of these youthful NDEers was adversely affected by the experience. In fact, they all seem to be somewhat better off.

Here are several case studies.

PATIENT ONE: "I SAW A LIGHT BULB IN MY BODY"

An eleven-year-old boy had been having blackout spells for several months. Finally, his parents brought him to Children's Hospital for an evaluation. While waiting in the lobby, he had another blackout followed by a cardiac arrest. Chaos erupted. Doctors rushed to the lobby and started mouth-to-mouth resuscitation and heart massage. He was then put on a gurney and rushed to the intensive care unit, where emergency procedures were begun to restart his heart.

He was without a heartbeat for at least twenty minutes. During this time, several cardiac medications were given, with no success. One of the nurses present remembers saying, "I wish we didn't have to do this," meaning that she thought the lifesaving attempts were useless.

As a last resort, the physicians tried the cardioversion paddles again. They pressed the devices against his chest and pushed the buttons that sent electrical current jolting through his heart. Miraculously, the boy opened his eyes and said, "That was weird. You sucked me back into my body!" He then lapsed back into unconsciousness.

The boy was taken to an operating room for emergency surgery. He had a condition called "sick sinus syndrome," in which the area of the heart that regulates the beating—the sinus node—stops working. An electrical pacemaker was implanted.

I spoke to the boy seven years later. He was in high school and worked at a part-time job. He had made a complete recovery from his cardiac arrest.

At first, he was very vague about this frightening experience. He didn't remember opening his eyes and speaking to the doctors and nurses after being brought back to life. He described the pain of the electric shock as "a pain I will never forget. I still have nightmares about the time that they put those paddles on my body."

Although his parents said that he didn't remember anything about that initial experience in the hospital waiting room, I sensed that this young man was somewhat troubled by his experience. I probed further, asking him for more details about that day and specifically about any dreams he might have had.

Finally, he looked me right in the eyes and said, "Well, if you promise not to laugh, I'll tell you what I remember. I still remember it as if it were yesterday.

"I remember going to the hospital that day. My parents had gone into a room [the admitting office], when suddenly I heard a whooshing sound in my ears. I felt like you feel when you go over a bump in a car going real fast, and you feel your stomach drop out. I heard a buzzing sound in my ears.

"The next thing I knew, I was in a room, crouched in a corner of the ceiling. I could see my body below me. It was real dark, you know. I could see my body because it was lit up with a light, like there was a light bulb inside me.

"I could see the doctors and nurses working on me. My doctor was there and so was Sandy, one of the nurses. I heard Sandy say, 'I wish we didn't have to do this.' I wondered what they were doing. I saw a doctor put jelly on my chest. My hair was really messed up. It seemed greasy, and I wished that I had washed my hair before coming to the hospital. They had cut my clothes off, but my pants were still on.

"I heard a doctor say, 'Stand back,' and then he pushed a button on one of the paddles. Suddenly, I was back inside my body. One minute I was looking down at my face. I could see the tops of the doctors' heads. After he pushed that button, I was suddenly looking into a doctor's face. Man, that hurt. It hurts just thinking about how much it hurts. I will never forget how much it hurt when the doctor pushed that button. I still have dreams about how much it hurt. Sometimes I wake up at night screaming from that pain.

"No, I have never heard of a near-death experience. I don't watch TV much. If I read, I read mostly comic books. No, I didn't tell my parents about it. I don't know why not; I guess I didn't feel like talking about it. I have never heard of anybody having this happen to them. I would not tell my friends about it. They would probably think I was crazy."

This young man had an out-of-body experience, one of the symptoms of the core experience. Typical of this, he saw his body illuminated by white light, while everything else seemed to be in darkness.

This patient didn't see this experience as an NDE. He considered it a dream. Despite that feeling, the experience transformed him, another result of the core experience. It is my observation that he now feels that he has a purpose in life. He is not overly interested in material things as so many of his friends are. He is more interested in acquiring knowledge than money. As he put it, "I don't feel like partying and drinking as much as my friends do or doing a lot of stupid stuff. I know that there is a better reason for living."

An interesting note about the NDE itself: He related many details about the experience that could be verified. He accurately described his own resuscitation, as though he really watched it from outside his body. An eleven-year-old cannot describe an emergency room resuscitation with any great accuracy, no matter how much television he watches. He was able to describe the positions and colors of the instruments around the room, the gender of the attending physicians, and even what they said during this frantic procedure.

PATIENT TWO: "I HAVE A WONDERFUL SECRET TO TELL YOU"

At the age of ten, Chris developed seriously high blood pressure from a kidney problem. The danger became so acute that doctors transplanted one of his mother's kidneys into his body.

After the transplant, a low-grade fever developed that his doctors couldn't control. Finally, wracked with stomach pain and losing strength, he was admitted to the hospital for further tests. The results were grim. Bacteria introduced into his body during the kidney transplant had invaded his heart, causing his aortic valve to swell.

Surgeons were forced to perform heart valve surgery, during which Chris "died" and was revived.

What he told me was substantiated by his mother, who had been at his bedside when he came out of surgery and told her this marvelous story, the same one he told me later.

"I woke up from surgery and there was my mom. I just couldn't wait to tell her what happened while

I was on the operating table. I said, 'I have a wonderful secret to tell you, Mother. I've been climbing a staircase to heaven.

"It was such a good and peaceful feeling. I felt wonderful. I was on a staircase, and it was dark, and I started climbing upward. I got about halfway up the staircase and decided not to go any higher. I wanted to go on up, but I knew I wouldn't come back if I went too high. That would hurt my mom and dad; since my little brother had already died, they wouldn't have anyone to take care of."

Chris then turned and went down the staircase. When he reached the bottom, he felt himself slip back into his body.

Months later Chris had completely forgotten this experience. When I tell him about it now, he smiles and shrugs as though it happened to someone else.

Chris just didn't forget the staircase. He had been treated with many narcotics and Valium, all of which cause amnesia. His case and those similar to it make me think that everyone who has almost died may possibly have had a near-death experience. Perhaps they frequently don't remember because the drugs given to them erase memory.

PATIENT THREE: "I WILL NEVER FORGET HIM"

Dean had very serious kidney problems that left him dependent on daily dialysis to clean his blood. After suffering from shortness of breath and disorientation, his parents took him to Children's Hospital. While in the admitting room, the sixteen-year-old suddenly slumped over in his chair. A nurse anxiously searched for his pulse but found none.

Dean was rushed to intensive care, where doctors started chest compression and injected epinephrine and other drugs to start his heart. These efforts worked. Twenty-four hours later, Dean was awake and fully oriented.

Dean told his doctors that he remembered leaving home and that was all. He told his family something more. He said that "I had an experience for which there are no human words that can be used to describe." When asked specifically what had happened, Dean would only say that he'd had a "supernatural experience."

That is how the issue was left until Dean entered my study two years later. We chatted about his treatment in the intensive care unit until he seemed to feel relaxed. Then I asked him if anything out of the ordinary had happened.

"It certainly did," he said. Then he told me about the angel.

"I was apparently lying on a table in the intensive care unit when I suddenly found myself standing up and traveling through a very wide tunnel. I couldn't see any walls on either side, but still I had the feeling that this was a tunnel. I also had the feeling that I was moving very fast even though there was no wind blowing on my face.

"I knew I was going somewhere, but I didn't know where. I knew there was something for me at the end of that tunnel, and I really wanted to get there. As far as I was concerned, there was nothing greater than what existed at the end of that tunnel. Forget my body, forget being alive, all I wanted to do was get to the end.

"I reached a certain point in the tunnel where lights suddenly began flashing all around me. They made me certain that I was in some kind of tunnel, and the way I moved past them, I knew I was going hundreds of miles an hour.

"At this point I also noticed that there was somebody with me. He was about seven feet tall and wore a long white gown with a simple belt tied at the waist. His hair was golden, and although he didn't say anything, I wasn't afraid because I could feel him radiating peace and love.

"No, he wasn't Christ, but I knew that he was sent from Christ. It was probably one of his angels or someone else sent to transport me to heaven."

Suddenly, Dean had the perception that he was back in his body again. He said he never really found out what was at the end of that tunnel, but he knew it was a very special destination. He also felt that the entire experience made him different from other people because it was so "supernatural."

"I had something happen to me that can't be described in words," said Dean. "I think I came back from this experience because I have a purpose in life."

Dean's experience was too profound for words. It was only after he had talked to other people he saw on a television show who had had NDEs that he realized what had happened. When he heard what they had to say about their NDEs, he was better able to verbalize his experience.

After listening to their son, Dean's family also believed that he had a calling. As a result of this experience, the entire family developed a deep faith in God.

I discovered later that Dean had had another near-death experience, at the age of ten. By that age, he had already had two kidney transplants and had spent hundreds of hours on dialysis machines.

One day, while swimming, he nearly drowned. All those hours of being hooked up to dialysis machines passed before his eyes. He also felt the physical pain of recovering from transplant surgery. "Oh no," he thought. "All that pain for nothing."

Dean then felt himself slip out of his body and become bathed in a bright white light.

"Something wonderful happened to me then, but I didn't really know what it was," he said to me.

Dean's first experience was interesting because it contained a life review, which is extremely rare among children or teenagers.

PATIENT FOUR: "EVERYTHING WAS WHITE"

Kurt was a seven-year-old with severe muscular dystrophy. Because of this disease, he was unable to breathe very well, and he needed to breathe oxygen from a tank to live.

Kurt became progressively sicker and finally developed pneumonia, which usually marks the end of an MD victim's life.

Near the end, he was in intensive care when his heart stopped. The doctors gave him closed heart massage, pushing on his chest with their palms, and restored his heartbeat. Still, he was completely without heartbeat for three minutes.

When I spoke to Kurt hours after his resuscitation, he was very much at peace. He knew he was going to die soon and seemed relieved to know his physical grief was nearing an end. His recent experience, Kurt said, had shown him a world without pain. When his heart had stopped beating, Kurt suddenly found himself outside his body watching the doctors and nurses work to revive him.

> "I saw Bonnie [one of the nurses present], and I said 'hi' to her," said Kurt. "Then everything became dark, until I saw angels. I was in a beautiful place with flowers and rainbows, where everything was white like it had its own light. I talked to several people while I was there, including Jesus, who wanted me to stay with him. I wanted to stay there, but we decided I had to come back and see my parents again. I'm not afraid to go back to that place."

I tried to get Kurt to draw what he had seen, but he was too weak to hold a pencil. He died a few weeks after we spoke.

I wish the family had been present at my interview to hear their son's description of what had happened to him. This interview took place in the emergency room at Children's Hospital. I did not feel comfortable telling his parents about the experience, and I know that the nurses who were present did not tell the family either. I have anguished over this case many times. I realize that I should have shared what I knew with Kurt's family. But neither I nor any of the other medical personnel present felt that a hospital environment allowed for a discussion of this kind. As one of the doctors present said: "For me to say to a family, 'and by the way, your son thought he went to heaven during the resuscitation,' would have made me feel like I was crazy. Medical school didn't teach me to talk about things like that."

Nonetheless, muscular dystrophy wastes a family just as it wastes the victim. Perhaps they should have been allowed to stay while their son was resuscitated. Knowing that their child had had an intense visionary experience before he died would have at least comforted them as they faced their son's imminent death.

PATIENT FIVE: "I MIGHT NOT COME BACK"

June, an eight-year-old girl, nearly drowned in a swimming pool when her hair became caught in the drain. Her parents, an emergency medical team, and finally emergency room doctors gave her CPR for more than forty-five minutes before her heart began beating again. She made a full neurological recovery in less than six weeks.

The story would have ended there had the bicycle

incident not happened. June was riding down her driveway toward the street when her mother shouted from the house for her to be careful. Distracted by her mother's voice, June rode into the street and was almost hit by a passing car.

"Did you want me to die again?" shouted June from across the street. "I might not come back next time."

June then told her mother what had happened when her life almost ended in the swimming pool. The story so worried June's mother that she asked her family doctor to refer them to a psychiatrist. Knowing my interest, the doctor instead referred them to me. Here is June's story:

"All I remember was my hair getting stuck in the drain and then blacking out. The next thing I knew, I floated out of my body. I could see myself under the water but I wasn't afraid. All of a sudden I started going up a tunnel, and before I could think about it, I found myself in heaven. I know it was heaven because everything was bright and everyone was cheerful.

"A nice man asked me if I wanted to stay there. I thought about staying; I really did. But I said 'I want to be with my family.' Then I got to come back."

This patient has full recall of the event. Not only does she remember its intense spiritual nature, but she can now totally recall the events of the resuscitation, from the time the paramedics reached her in the back-yard to the work done on her in the emergency room.

PATIENT SIX: "IT WOULD BE WRONG TO PUSH THE BUTTON"

Eight-year-old Michelle was taken to the emergency room by her mother, who said she had been feeling ill and acting extremely disoriented. After giving a urine sample to a nurse, Michelle became unresponsive and then quickly slipped into unconsciousness. Through her urine sample and other tests, doctors determined that the little girl was in a diabetic coma. She had the highest blood sugar level ever recorded at this hospital.

She remained in a deep coma for several days before awakening with stories of drifting out of her body and being given the chance to choose her fate by the push of a button.

When I spoke to Michelle, at my office at Children's Hospital several weeks after her recovery, she didn't want to talk about her coma experience. She shyly avoided the subject, shrugging her shoulders when I asked her if there was anything special she remembered while in the hospital. It wasn't until I gave her a piece of paper and crayons to draw what had happened that she began to loosen up and talk about her memories of being on the threshold of death. She said that when she lost consciousness she had been feeling very nauseous and dizzy:

"All of a sudden I was floating above my body looking down at myself. There were two doctors pushing me on one of those stretchers toward a room. Both were women doctors. I felt funny. I was sick and my head hurt when my mom brought me in, but when I was floating, I didn't feel bad. I felt good.

Her mother, who was present, told me there was more to the story, but once again Michelle didn't want to talk. I gave her another piece of paper and said she could draw what had happened if she wanted to. She did. As her crayon drew people in white, she began to talk about the second part of her near-death experience. The emotion of the experience weighed heavily on Michelle. She told her story slowly, not looking up from the paper as she talked:

"I was somewhere lying down. Behind me were a whole bunch of people in white. They were talking to me. In front of me were two buttons, a red one and a green one. The people in white kept telling me to push the red button. But I knew I should push the green one because the red button would mean I wouldn't come back. I pushed the green one instead and woke up from the coma. I don't know why I knew that the red button was bad. But it was, because I'm still here."

This event contains several elements of the near-death experience. For one thing, she is out of her body. She is able to provide excellent details about what happened during her resuscitation. Such details as the positions of instruments and the number of people in the room are all described accurately by Michelle.

She also had to make a decision to return to the

body, which is another core element of the near-death experience. In fact, fifty percent of the children in my study made some sort of decision to return to the body. For Michelle, it was the pushing of a button. For others, it is being asked whether or not they want to return. Another child told me that after major heart surgery a lady dressed in white teased her and tried to make her follow her down a long sidewalk. The girl decided to come back when she became tired of walking. In all instances, a conscious decision to return is present. In adult studies, only about twenty percent of the patients made a conscious decision to return.

Michelle saw beings in white, another core element. She describes them as doctors instead of "beings of light." When I asked her why she thought they were doctors, she answered that they were "big and dressed in white and I was scared of them."

Although her interpretation is different, she has all the elements of an NDE.

PATIENT SEVEN: "I CRAWLED UP THE TUNNEL"

Mark's story is among the most fascinating near-death experiences because of his age when it happened—he was only nine months old. It wasn't until he was three that Mark told his parents about his remarkable experience. His recall was amazing for two reasons. For one, most people don't remember anything from that age. For another, Mark had never been told of his cardiac arrest by his parents.

At the age of nine months, Mark had severe bronchiolitis. While in the emergency room, he had a full cardiopulmonary arrest. For more than forty minutes, doctors worked to revive him and finally did. Most people show signs of mental retardation from experiences such as this, but not Mark. He had a full recovery and has shown normal growth and development since crossing the threshold of death.

Mark first mentioned his near-death experience when he was three years old. Then, following a Christmas pageant, he said that God didn't look like the man in the play they had just seen. When his father asked him what he meant, Mark told him what had happened during that frantic night two years earlier:

> "I saw nurses and doctors standing over me trying to wake me up. I flew out of the room and [went to the waiting room, where I] saw Grandpa and Grandma crying and holding each other. I think they thought I was going to die."

He then reported seeing a long, dark tunnel and crawling up it. He said it was difficult to crawl without a helping hand, but he couldn't say who was helping him. At the end of this tunnel was a bright light that kept him going.

At the end of that tunnel, he found a "bright place" and "ran through fields with God." He was very animated when he described this run with God. He said that "one can double jump in heaven" (a statement, incidentally, that I heard later from another patient) and run without effort.

God then asked if he wanted to go "back home." Mark said "no," but God told him he would come back again some other day.

Mark remembered his experience vividly until the age of five, when doctors removed the trachea tube they had inserted to remedy a problem known as tracheomalacia, or floppy windpipe. Then the memory of the experience began to fade. I suspect that the removal of the trachea signaled his subconscious that he was no longer in danger of dying, and he began to lose memory. Now, Mark is a well-adjusted teenager who has high hopes of becoming a physical therapist or athletic trainer.

At first, most people are skeptical of this story. As one colleague said: "A nine-month-old child crawling to heaven? Give me a break." Still, could a nine-month-old remember a near-death experience? The answer is yes.

Recent research indicates that learning and memory begins much earlier than previously thought. In one research project, seven-month-olds watched a videotape showing them how to fit a toy together. The researchers then gave those pieces to the children, who were then able to assemble the toy as a result of what they had learned from the video. In the control group, children were given the pieces without first seeing the video and were unable to fit the toy together.

PATIENT EIGHT: "SPARKS WOULD FILL THE AIR"

Cindi's is a story of the eighties. She is a seventeen-year-old who was kicked out of her home at the age of fifteen and has since lived with her boyfriend. An infrequent drug user, one night she smoked crack (a crystal form of cocaine) and then complained of severe chest pains. By the time her boyfriend drove her to the hospital, she was in complete cardiac arrest.

Doctors worked to resuscitate her for several hours, even opened her chest and administered cardiac massage. Although normal heartbeat was restored, Cindi lay comatose for several hours.

Finally, her family doctor, Vern Cherewatenko, arrived and spoke to her. "You can't give up," he told her. "You have to fight. We've done all we can, and now it's up to you." He then asked her to open her eyes and talk to him. After several seconds, her eyelids fluttered and she awoke.

I spoke to Cindi a couple of weeks after her brush with death. She told me of a spiritual journey that led to a meeting with her long-dead grandfather.

"I passed out in the car. The next thing I remember was floating above my body and watching the doctors pushing on my chest. I now know that they were inside my chest, but I couldn't see that. All I could see was them working on me, and I couldn't really see any of the details.

"I then passed into a room filled with all of my friends. The room was very large and open at the top. It was like looking out at the sky. Sparks would fill the air and streaks of light zoomed up from the earth and burst into rainbows. I wanted very much to be one of those sparks, but I didn't know how to lift myself up and become one.

"I wanted to leave the room, but the door was closed. I knew if I opened it, I could never return. I was afraid of the door but wanted to go through it too, if you know what I mean.

"My dead grandfather then came to help me. He was a very religious man. He took me by the hand and said, 'Go back to your body. You have work to do.' Then he led me out of the room and back to my body. The next thing I remember, I was awake."

Cindi's experience is classic in its content. She sees a roomful of people, has contact with her dead grandfather. She experiences a barrier in the form of a door. She knows that if she opens it she will not return to her body.

One might wonder about the return aspect of this near-death experience. When her family doctor whispered in her ear that the decision to return is up to her, could his voice somehow have become mixed up in her mind with that of her dead grandfather's? Possibly, but whoever was responsible, she responded well.

PATIENT NINE: "I WAS FLOATING ABOVE MY BODY"

Linda was thirteen years old when she had a severe asthma attack that led to a cardiopulmonary arrest.

The day before her asthma attack, she had taken several oral medications and had used the inhalant as often as every half hour to overcome her wheezing.

About midnight she awoke and asked for more medication, which her parents gave her. Several hours later, she woke up screaming. By the time her parents got to her room, Linda had stopped breathing and was blue from lack of oxygen. Her father began administering mouth-to-mouth resuscitation until a medical unit arrived and injected her with epinephrine, which restored her breathing. She was then moved to the hospital.

Linda was not at all reluctant to talk about her experience. When I asked her what she remembered, she was quick to tell me:

> "It was a funny feeling. I was in a lot of pain before I blacked out. Then all of a sudden I was looking down at my body! But at the same time, it wasn't like I was really out of my body looking down. I was in it and out of it at the same time.
>
> "I couldn't see anything that was being done to my body. I couldn't see the rest of the room or anything. All I could see was myself lying on the floor. Also I had a very peaceful feeling, like nothing had really happened to me at all."

After her brief out-of-body excursion, Linda didn't remember anything else until she arrived at the hospital.

She found the experience to be interesting but not particularly meaningful. Several times during the interview, Linda said that she felt lucky to have had the experience and lucky to be alive.

PATIENT TEN: "I LOOKED YUCKY"

Six-year-old Daniel was struck by a car while riding his bicycle and received a severe head trauma. He was comatose for two weeks. He remembers almost nothing of the accident or of the moments before. He says he remembers taking his bicycle out of the garage and riding down the driveway. His most vivid remembrance is what happened after he was struck:

> "I was standing there watching the doctors load me into the ambulance, when I saw that I was outside my body. My mom was crying and everyone was in a hurry.
>
> "When I got to the hospital, I watched the doctors put tubes in me. I looked yucky because I was bloody and bruised.
>
> "I then went down a tunnel that was dark. At the end of the tunnel was a bright light. I wasn't sad and I wasn't happy, but I did want to get to the Light. When I got to it, I met three men. One was very tall and the other two were short. Behind them was a rainbow bridge that stretched across the sky. They seemed nice, but I was afraid of them anyway.
>
> "All of a sudden I was back in my body. I looked down at my feet, and the men were there. Then they disappeared, and I was completely back."

This experience made Daniel believe that other worlds exist. It was also somewhat frightening for him because he thought that these men were going to take him to a place away from his parents. "They seemed nice," Daniel told me. "But I didn't want to leave my mom and dad."

PUBLISH AND PERISH

My study was published November 1986 in the *American Journal of Diseases of Children*, the American Medical Association's pediatric journal. It proved—as no other study before—that a person must be on the brink of death to have the symptoms of an NDE. My findings eliminated the theory that NDEs are the result of drugs or sleep deprivation or that they are merely bad dreams or the subconscious awareness of surgery.

Think about it. Of the 121 patients we interviewed who had survived a serious illness but were not near death, 118 had no experience at all. The remaining three had dreams of white-coated monsters and the like.

Meanwhile, eight of the twelve survivors of heart attacks had visions of leaving their bodies and traveling to other realms. That is almost seventy percent, a percentage so high it eliminates the element of chance or statistical error. In addition, I did not permit anyone to volunteer for the study. Instead, I interviewed over a ten-year period survivors of cardiac arrest. Doing that prevented children from entering the study who might have made up a story just to be included.

I also thoroughly reviewed the medical records of all patients I studied, carefully documenting the drugs they were on, the anesthesia used, the amount of oxygen in their blood, and the results of various laboratory tests. I carefully matched my control patients and those in the study group to make sure they were the same age. I also made sure that both groups were intubated, or attached to an artificial lung machine.

The reason for this matching was to see if near-death experiences are hallucinations caused by drugs or lack of oxygen in the blood as many physicians believe. The answer is that they are not. Many of the patients who had full-blown near-death experiences were not being treated with any hallucinogenic medications at all. The control group had nothing resembling near-death experiences despite being treated with such drugs as morphine, Valium, and Thorazine and such anesthetic agents as Dilantin, phenobarbital, mannitol, and codeine. The patients were also hypoxic, had acid-base balance disturbances, and had high CO_2 levels, and every combination you could imagine. Yet they had nothing we could call an NDE.

To make sure I wasn't missing anything, I had a team of medical students comb the psychological and medical literature in search of drugs, psychological states, or oxygen-deprivation states that caused hallucinations similar to NDEs. Ketamine and LSD came the closest, but neither of these drugs is used in normal patient care nor were they used on either my control or study group.

Most researchers are faced with the problem of "publish or perish." In my case, I published *and* perished. Three articles on the Seattle study were published in the American Medical Association's prestigious pediatric journal. The scientists and physicians who reviewed my protocol were very complimentary about my research design and the scientific validity of the results.

I did not sensationalize the results in any way. Although I knew this research would be of great interest to the general public, I felt that any publicity might leave me open to charges that I was trying to benefit personally from the research. I assumed that physicians would be intensely interested in these results, and they were. I received requests for reprints of the articles from around the world as well as phone calls from colleagues who were excited to read our results and who had encountered similar cases in their own practices.

The study showed that near-death experiences are seen in the great majority of critically ill children and clearly have some association with the dying process. It also revealed that these experiences are clearly not caused by drugs, but are a natural psychological process associated with dying.

These results had not even been tested for in the studies of the near-death experience conducted by Dr. Raymond Moody and others.

I was fortunate that the editors of the *American Journal of Diseases of Children* were open-minded enough to publish our research. I emphasized in my conclusion that these experiences are probably a natural part of the dying process and as such are worthy of study. I have never asserted that they are proof of life after death nor do I feel that a hospital is the proper place to study religion and metaphysics.

I made the point that people die in hospitals and that therefore the dying process should be examined in hospitals.

Unfortunately, the hospital's Human Subject Review Committee didn't agree with me. They suddenly and mysteriously refused to let me continue with the same research that three years earlier had been approved with the proclamation that mine was "the most interesting research project we have reviewed in a long time."

I was crushed. I returned to the committee and asked for $3,000 to proceed with the second phase of the Seattle study. The plan was to study Asian immigrants to the Seattle area to see what children from a different culture experience at the point of death.

This time the committee said that such a study would be too intrusive on patient's rights. By making them relive these traumatic events, I was causing unnecessary suffering.

I pointed out that the opposite had been true. The patients actually appreciated a doctor showing interest in their experience. And besides, participation was voluntary. Subjects were told that they didn't have to talk unless they wanted to.

The answer from the committee was "No." I couldn't even get permission to informally study these patients.

I feel that intruding on patient's rights had nothing to do with the decision. The real reason, I feel, is that doctors don't like to research death. Although most people die in hospitals, the subject of death is almost taboo there.

I remember the head of my research program asking me why I was researching near-death experiences. I told him that although much was known about infant colic and toilet training relatively little was known about the dying process. I simply wanted to know what happened at the point of death.

When I said that, he shook his head. "But what are you really trying to do?"

3

Predeath Visions

The greater the ignorance, the greater the dogmatism.
—*Sir William Osler, M.D.*

Just what *was* I trying to do? Trying to comprehend what happens beyond the great divide? Hoping to help patients cope with a rapidly approaching death?

Both those things, actually. The medical establishment wears mental blinders when it comes to the subject of death. In some respects, it should be that way. After all, a patient expects life from his physician. He expects healing for his sickness, comfort for his ailments. He expects success since failure usually means pain. But doctors should be able to answer questions about death just as we can about other aspects of normal development and life stages.

In many ways, the physician is as poorly equipped to handle failure as is the patient. For instance, it is well documented that as patients get closer to death their doctors spend less time at their bedsides.

Time and motion studies in intensive care units show that as patients become sicker physicians spend more time performing procedures and much less time examining the patient or providing psychological comfort. Part of the reason that many doctors don't want to work with AIDS patients is the depressing fact that so far there is a zero rate of recovery from the disease.

In five years of residency training, I had only one lecture on death and dying that explained how to deal with the emotions and stresses that working with dying patients may generate. In that lecture, I was given an "excellent formula" with which to talk to parents about the events surrounding the death of a child to make sure that they understood that everything that should have been done was done. I was also told to explain that they might hear their child after he has died and that these "hallucinations" should resolve themselves in three to six weeks.

Soon I changed this formula to a more palatable one. I simply told the grieving parents that they would hear their child's voice again and not to let it worry or distress them. After making this change, I began to get the most wonderful thank-you letters from parents. Telling them the simple truth—that they would hear their child's voice again—but not labeling it an hallucination, gave dignity to the experience.

Other than that formula, we were given no tools to help people cope with the angst of death. This is especially bad since death is something a physician is forced to deal with early in a medical career. Most of us are just out of medical school when we face the all too frequent failures of medicine. The lesson stated by my partner, Dr. David Christopher, that "medicine is great, but not that great" is a hard one for a doctor to learn.

I learned my first and harshest lesson about death after serving as an intern for only three days. I was working in the infant intensive care unit when one of the patients died. The weeping parents took their baby into a small room to be alone with him in their grief.

The baby hadn't died suddenly. Another intern and I had spent three hours trying to save him. We had started resuscitation at the end of a thirty-six-hour shift and were exhausted when it was finally all over. It was my first hands-on cardiac arrest, and it didn't seem real to me. Though absolutely worn-out, we were filled with the excitement and adrenaline that such an intense experience can generate.

In our exhaustion, we made the ghoulish jokes that callow interns sometimes make. We laughed and spoke loudly about what a great case this had been. "I got to put in three chest tubes and an arterial line," my partner bragged to one of the nurses. In the midst of this shamefully boisterous conversation, the parents came out of the room.

The shame hit me so hard I almost lost my breath. The nurses covered their mouths and walked away slowly. The other intern and I were left alone in the hallway to face the parents. The heavy weight of shame that I felt prevented me from looking the sad couple in the eyes.

Gently they took our hands and thanked us for what

we had done to save their son. The mother then spoke
to one of the nurses. "We heard your laughter and at
first we were angry. We were shocked that you would
be laughing at a time like this. Then we suddenly
found ourselves enjoying the sound of your laughter.
We knew that we suffered the loss of our son, but that
life and joy still existed in the world. Thank you for
your laughter and thank you for trying to save our
son."

To avoid thinking about death, I turned to the technical skills of medicine, taking my joy from placing
lines in patients and reading machines. I never questioned the need to resuscitate a patient. Most of us
believed in doing everything medically possible to save
patients. When I was a doctor with Airlift Northwest,
we transported many people who had no chance of
survival to hospitals. Some were victims of automobile accidents. Others were patients of private physicians who didn't want them to die in their community
hospital. Whatever the case, these patients were never
permitted to die en route. They were kept alive and
typically would die hours or days later. Even then,
they were often attached to life-sustaining machines
and actually needed "permission" from relatives to
die.

Our job was to follow the motto "every patient
deserves the absolute best care possible." I never
questioned that the "best care" meant aggressive
intervention at the point of death to revive the patient.
I still don't question that credo.

The physician's dilemma is, where to draw the line?

In his book *New Meanings of Death*, Herman Feifel
recounts how Americans die isolated deaths in hospitals today. "Dying and death are now the province of
the professional, i.e., the physician. Unfortunately, too
many of them tend to use their professional knowledge
as a buffer against unprotected encounters with death
to bind their own anxieties. Accordingly, when the
physician is called upon to blunt the edge of grief, to
interpret death to family, he is usually unsuccessful."

So just what *was* I trying to do with this study? *I
was trying to understand the near-death experience*
was my answer to the skeptical chief of research.

As one of my medical professors said of the human
body, "If you don't understand it, you can't explain
it." The same is true of death and the near-death experience. All I was trying to do was understand it.

UNDERGROUND INTEREST

The cold reception the Seattle study received from
some of my colleagues did little to stifle my interest.
I continued to collect stories of patients' near-death
experiences from other doctors who knew of my interest and were curious themselves.

Hardly a week went by without a doctor or nurse
telling me a puzzling story about a patient having a
detailed out-of-body experience or about someone being revived from near death only to tell of a world of
light and beauty on the other side. I listened, took
notes, and then interviewed the patient to verify the
details.

These predeath visions are intensely real experiences that a dying person has while still conscious. Reality is not distorted or altered. The dying patient often sees God, angels, dead relatives or visions of heaven superimposed upon reality or actually present at the deathbed. The experiences are considered mystical and visionary in content and resemble NDEs.

A fascinating category of experiences began to emerge from these referrals, a phenomenon other researchers have called *predeath visions*.

Karlis Osis and Erlendur Haraldsson, two psychologists who collected many case studies of visions at the hour of death, have done the most extensive work in this field. They have found that these predeath visions have many things in common with near-death experiences. For instance, the dying patient who has been in pain for several days suddenly finds himself devoid of pain and discomfort, a trait similar to people having near-death experiences. Also, predeath visions frequently involve visions of other worlds and conversations with dead loved ones.

Osis and Haraldsson have stated that the predeath visions they collected usually occurred to unsedated patients whose minds were clear a few hours before death. The contents differed widely, but they were dominated by deceased relatives and friends who the patients perceived as coming to take them away. Here is one example of a predeath vision that was reported by a nurse who was at the deathbed of a man in his forties:

"He was unsedated, fully conscious, and had a low temperature. He was a rather religious person and believed in life after death. We expected him to die, and he probably did too, as he was asking us to pray for him. In the room where he was lying, there was a staircase leading to the second floor. Suddenly he exclaimed: 'See, the angels are coming down the stairs. The glass has fallen and broken.' All of us in the room looked toward the staircase where a drinking glass had been placed on one of the steps. As we looked, we saw the glass break into a thousand pieces without any apparent cause. It did not fall; it simply exploded. The angels, of course, we did not see. A happy and peaceful expression came over the patient's face, and the next moment he expired. Even after his death, the serene, peaceful expression remained on his face."

In another predeath vision from the research of Osis and Haraldsson, a doctor recalls the experience of a seriously ill patient:

"The condition [of the man] suffering from a heart attack had been serious for the last few days. Suddenly he gained consciousness. He looked better and cheerful. He talked nicely to his relatives and requested them to go home. He also said, 'I shall go to my home. Angels have come to take me away.' He looked relieved and cheerful."

After years of studying these visions, Osis and Haraldsson have concluded that predeath visions and neardeath experiences are one in the same. I am inclined to agree with their assessment that the difference between the two is in terminology only. The following two cases are typical of what I encountered. In many ways, the first could be called a "prelife" vision in that the patient had a vision of remission from what would normally be a fatal disease.

Six-year-old Derek was dying of a type of tumor called a "neuroblastoma," or at least that is what the doctors thought. He had been in the hospital for several weeks, and his rapid deterioration indicated a very grim prognosis. At best, Derek was expected to live only about a month longer.

Derek had an entirely different notion of what would happen. One day, he drew a picture of himself in which the tumor disappeared. He told his doctor that he'd had a vision the night before in which the tumor left his body. Although his doctor insisted it was merely a dream, Derek claimed it was much more than that. He said it was real.

Derek proved to be right. From that day on, the boy improved until he had a complete remission of his disease.

The opposite was true in another case. A young girl, Becky, was told by her physicians that chemotherapy had worked and that she was going to survive her brain tumor. All of their high-tech medical tests said it was so.

That night, she had a vision in which a woman in white told her that she was going to die. Her doctor insisted that it was only a dream. Becky knew that it was real, she said. The vision was as clear as though people had come into the room and had spoken to her. Within weeks she deteriorated and died.

I quickly realized that a death experience presents a dilemma for the person who has it and everyone around them as well.

JOHN'S PREVIEW OF HEAVEN

For thousands of years, predeath visions were accepted as part of the dying process. Before death became the domain of the hospital, these visions were common and expected.

French historian Philippe Ariès has documented that before 1000 A.D. people had entirely different death experiences than the ones we have today. When the dying person felt his time was near he usually reviewed his life, his achievements and failures, and wept for the sorrow he felt in knowing he wouldn't see family or friends again. The dying person then asked forgiveness of friends and family for any trespasses he might have committed in the life he was about to leave. Usually, says Ariès, the dying would tell of visions of God and of seeing those who had died before them.

How different dying is today. Patients who have predeath visions are treated for "anxiety" with narcotics and Valium, both of which erase short-term memory and prevent patients from remembering any visions or near-death experiences they may have had.

These visions are a forgotten aspect of life's mysterious process. A case like John's illustrates that predeath visions can reduce pain—for the patient and the family.

John was an eleven-year-old patient of mine who was dying of lymphoma. In his last days, he was hospitalized with severe, untreatable pneumonia. Though he was having difficulty breathing and was in constant pain, he was given very few drugs such as morphine and Valium because they make breathing more difficult.

Three days before John died, a circle of loved ones gathered around his bed. They were startled when John suddenly sat upright and announced that Jesus was in the room. He then asked for everyone to pray for him.

At about three A.M., John sat up again, startling the four people who had gathered around the bed to pray. "There are beautiful colors in the sky!" he shouted. "There are beautiful colors and more colors. You can double jump up here, double jump!"

At four A.M. an extraordinary event occurred. They were joined by a woman who said that she had received a strong premonition that she had to visit John right away. She was not known to John's parents, but her son was a playmate of John's. She had no explanation for why she would suddenly visit John at four A.M. except to explain that she had had a vivid dream about John and had felt a need to visit him that was overpowering.

By dawn, it seemed that life was almost over for John. His breathing was labored, and his heart was pounding like that of a marathon runner's. Even then, little John had more to communicate. Opening his eyes wide, he asked his grieving parents to "let me go."

"Don't be afraid," he said. "I've seen God, angels, and shepherds. I see the white horse."

As sick as he was, John still begged his family not to feel sorry for him. He had seen where he was going, and it was a joyous and wondrous place. "It's wonderful. It's beautiful," he said, his hand held out in front of him.

Soon he laid back and fell asleep. John never regained consciousness and died two days later.

John's visions and the incidents surrounding them intrigued me. John's mother believes that through God's mediation, John communicated with his friend's mother. Although she knew he had been hospitalized, it was during the period of his most powerful visions that she had her vision of John. Although I have nothing scientific to base this on, I think coincidence was too great for these periods of "vision activity" not to be connected in some way.

Paranormal occurrences aside, John's beautiful visions consoled his family. By reassuring his parents that he was going to a joyous and wondrous place with God, John brought his family closer together. Instead of suffering the shattering loss that so many families experience when they lose a child, John's family left the hospital knowing that they had done everything they could to save their son. They also firmly believed that he was safely at rest in God's hands.

John died a rare death in the world of modern medicine. He had taken no painkillers, no mind-altering medications; he was surrounded by family and friends. His visions left his family intact and comforted. I would have thought that this experience would generate tremendous interest in the healing aspects of predeath visions. After all, if he'd had a unique medical problem—even an unusual rash—his case would have been presented throughout the hospital.

Yet his visions and their healing effects on the family were never mentioned by nurses or physicians. It wasn't that we didn't believe they had happened. We just didn't know how to respond to them. A rash can be seen by everyone, but a vision belongs to the experiencer alone.

The one time I did hear another physician mention John's visions was when a new resident said that they were probably caused by a lack of oxygen. He said that they could have been "cured" by increasing John's morphine intake. To him, the visions were seen as a problem to be medicated away, not as a solution. About ninety percent of people who die in hospitals are heavily sedated, endlessly resuscitated and medicated until even the most aggressive physician has had enough, and the body is permitted to die.

When patients experience visions, doctors often repress them with medication and then flee to the comfort of their other, less sick patients. Nothing in medical school ever prepared them to do anything else.

MIKE'S SUBURBAN DEATH

Mike was a bright fourteen-year-old who was dying of cystic fibrosis, a genetic disease in which the lungs become filled with scar tissue and eventually stop functioning. During his last days, his private physician asked me to pay a home visit to share what I knew about the process of dying. Mike had chosen to die at home, a decision supported by his family, who didn't want to see him hooked up to machines that would only belabor his death.

Mike's recent "hallucinations" had been giving them second thoughts about home care. He was experiencing "a different reality," according to his mother, one that was similar to ours, but still "terrifying and confusing." His doctor had prescribed chloral hydrate, a mild sedative, but it had little effect on the hallucinations. They kept coming with greater frequency and intensity. Mike spoke to me on the telephone the day before I visited and told me about them. "We have to talk about them when you get here," he said.

The next day I drove to the affluent Seattle suburb where Mike would die. I admired his parent's home and the well-kept grounds that gave no hint of the mortality that lurked behind its manicured hedges. How difficult it must have been for these parents to allow their son to die at home.

I spent about two hours in the living room talking with Mike's family about these "horrible hallucinations." They didn't think it would be this difficult,

said his mother. They had pictured him dying quietly
and peacefully at home, not "troubled by terrible visions." They did not think that their son's visions were
supernatural or natural in any way. They thought that
they were caused by a combination of medication and
delirium. Even his social worker asked me if I could
"take these hallucinations away." His physician and I
discussed what drugs might suppress these experiences.

Then I went in and talked to Mike. His perception
of the hallucinations was very different. After talking
to him for almost two hours I realized that he was
actually having beautiful and wondrous predeath visions. These weren't frightening or painful experiences for him at all. Instead, they contained a message
of healing and hope for his family and comfort for
himself in his final days.

Mike lay in bed and told me about things that only
he could see:

"The visions come when I am awake. They scare
me because I don't know when they will end and
how they will stop. It scares me because I don't
know reality. I see my reflection in the television
set, and I know I am here. I feel my hair, and I
know I am here. Then the visions start.

"In them, there are lots of people in the room.
God is here too. He is in control, but sometimes he
lets me be in control with him. There is bright light
and people all around. But then I come out of it and
I am Mike Smith and I am mortal.

"There is a religious part to these visions too. I
can sometimes see a cross of light."

It became clear that Mike wasn't afraid of the visions, just confused by them. In this stressful situation, Mike's parents were reacting to this confusion with fear of their own. Mike and I devised a plan. We developed cues that would help him distinguish between reality and vision. That way, instead of being frightened by what was happening, Mike could have some control over the situation by at least knowing where he was. He bashfully revealed one very poignant cue from his other world: Mike could have an erection, a very important event to him (as it is to most teenagers). He had never had an erection or orgasm because of the ravages of his disease. Only in his "other world" could he have them.

These cues gave Mike a feeling of mastery over the experiences. He began to relax and interpret them for his family. His calm changed the nature of these events for the family. Rather than thinking he was delirious (which he wasn't), his family was comforted by his visions. Instead of the frightening episodes they once were, his parents now wanted to know what he was seeing.

Six days before he passed away, the dreams became more frequent and intense. He reported almost daily that he saw bright lights, other people, and another land. He always mentioned that God was present in these visions. Although the parents didn't believe that Mike was actually visiting God, his visions helped them accept their son's death.

His peace with himself eased his parents' pain. The family had been torn by his impending death. Now he was bringing it back together with his acceptance of what was to be. He told us of the significant losses in his life, of not going to school or summer camp, of never having kissed a girl. He urged his parents to share their emotions with each other. He even gave his brother permission to go off to college without feeling guilty that he was at home dying.

From the time I met him, Mike looked forward to becoming "one with God" in his visions. "When I become one with God, the dreams will be over and I will be dead." That finally happened. Peacefully. It made me glad I hadn't taken those visions away from him.

TECHNICAL SKILLS AND HUMAN UNDERSTANDING

I am not presenting these predeath visions as a way of saying that medication should be withheld from dying patients. Nor am I criticizing doctors who want to prolong life even when things seem hopeless. Indeed, I am one of those physicians. I have resuscitated dozens of patients. I have seen miraculous full recoveries in patients for whom I thought there would be no tomorrow. The fact that we are now hearing thousands of cases of near-death experiences is testimony to our improved ability to snatch patients from the jaws of death.

There comes a time when the doctor must close his black bag, take the stethoscope out of his ears, *and* listen to his patient. As Dr. Tinsley Randolph

Harrison so eloquently put it in *Harrison's Principles of Internal Medicine*: "In the treating of suffering, there is need for technical skill, scientific knowledge and human understanding."

I advocate listening to the dying patient. Rather than making the wrong assumptions about the meaning of these predeath visions, we should analyze what we are attempting to achieve when we routinely place dying patients on drugs "to make them comfortable." We should learn new routines and forge different attitudes that incorporate this new information about death and dying. By changing these attitudes, we can learn new methods of allowing patients to die in control and with dignity.

We physicians can also learn to treat the dying with dignity. It's no coincidence that time and motion studies show doctors spending less time with a patient as he nears death. Doctors like to think they are in control of situations. When a patient starts slipping away, the physician can feel uncomfortable with a situation he can't control. Physicians sometimes fear becoming involved with a patient. Feeling emotionally close to a patient means that the doctor too will suffer an emotional loss when the patient dies.

I mentioned earlier a "formula" we were taught in medical school to help parents cope with the death of a child and at the same time help us stay uninvolved. I was lucky enough to have a mentor during my pediatric residency show me the fallacy of that formula.

I had just witnessed a healthy newborn die of an overwhelming infection at birth. The baby was literally healthy one minute and dying the next. Preliminary blood tests had hinted that something terrible was wrong. Before we had time to act, the baby deteriorated and died.

The older, more experienced physician and I went into the room to talk with the parents. I was filled with anxiety. I felt like a failure. I agonized about our inability to act fast enough and felt personally responsible for the death of this infant. How could I look at the parents and deliver the formula speech? Even though babies with this kind of infection almost always die, how could I tell them we had tried? I felt haunted by my failure.

To my surprise, my mentor didn't use a formula. He simply told them that their baby had died and that we had tried our best to save him.

He then started to cry.

We all sat in this starkly simple hospital room and cried together. Finally, he dried his eyes and said that there were other patients to see. He kissed them both, and we left.

This compassionate doctor showed me that it is possible to share the terror and grief of death with the patient. He was thinking of them and their loss, and they felt it. His tears were more reassuring than all my logical explanations of how a newborn is an immunocompromised host, a potential breeding ground for infection.

I had another such experience as a resident.

I was caring for a twenty-four-year-old man who was dying of leukemia. He insisted upon a regimen in which he would take his chemotherapy for several months and then leave the hospital before all of the cancer had been purged from his body. He would then return to his profession, which was teaching young children how to ride horses. When asked why he refused to complete a six-month course of chemotherapy, he replied, "I don't want to spend my whole life being sick. I've got to get back to work."

I was frustrated by his approach to treatment. I pleaded with him to finish an entire series of the chemotherapy and not quit before the healing process was complete. There was no question in my mind that this cavalier attitude was greatly shortening his life.

As angry as I was with this patient, I still liked him. He was the same age as I and took great pleasure in his work. His greatest concern was that his students learn proper riding techniques and enjoy it in the process. He seemed least concerned about his own well-being. I used to tell him that I liked him more than he liked himself.

He was in terrible shape when he came into the hospital for the last time. We both knew that this was the last round of chemotherapy he would attempt and that the cancer he refused to take seriously had finally won. He said that he only wanted to live two more weeks so he could see his students in their graduation ceremonies.

I was grief stricken by his impending death, but thought I concealed those feelings behind a wall of professionalism. I was wrong. During grand rounds one day, the attending physician asked him how he felt about dying. He startled me by saying, "I know I'm going to die pretty soon, and I'm okay with that. But what are we going to do about Mel here? How is he going to handle it?"

I never handled it at all. One of the attending physicians talked to me about the dangers of overidentifying with patients. He didn't mention the sense of defeat that death brings to the doctor. He only offered advice on how to stay in control during any situation.

"IT'S MY TIME TO DIE"

This story involves an event I didn't witness. It was told to me by a physician in Utah.

A five-year-old boy was in a coma, dying from a malignant brain tumor. He had been in the coma for three weeks and was surrounded almost the entire time by his family. They encircled his bed and prayed constantly for his recovery, taking only brief breaks to eat and rest.

At the end of the third week, the pastor of the family's church came into the hospital room and told them a remarkable story. He'd had a dream, he said, in which the boy told him, "It's my time to die. You must tell my parents to quit praying. I am supposed to go now."

The pastor was nervous about delivering this message to the family. Still, he said, it was a message too vivid to ignore. "It's as though he was right there in the room, talking to me face to face."

The family members accepted the minister's dream

as a message from their son. They prayed, they touched his comatose body, and they told him that he would be missed, but he had permission to die.

Suddenly, the boy regained consciousness. He thanked his family for letting him go and told them he would be dying soon. He died the next day.

Perhaps the most important aspect of this story is its cathartic nature. This family was allowed to assuage its grief because they knew that their son was ready to die. Their resentment of life's process and of God's will was replaced by the assurance that something mystical had taken place.

"I WON'T BE HERE MUCH LONGER"

The healing nature of predeath visions is evident in another experience that a man named Ted told me about his daughter. She was dying of cystic fibrosis at the age of sixteen. While lying awake in the hospital, she had a brief vision of a bright light and a glowing man who kindly beckoned her toward him.

When her family returned to her hospital room, they noticed an air of peace around her that had not been present before. "I have seen a beautiful light," she said. "I won't be here much longer."

The girl's predeath vision transformed the deathbed scene from the grueling nightmare it had become to one of joy and love. She talked with her family about the experience and prepared them for her death.

The father said that the atmosphere lightened after the daughter spoke of her experience and of the death that would soon follow. The nurses cried and hugged one another, and the burden of guilt that parents feel was lifted.

Without the predeath vision and the discussion it inspired, the healing process would have taken much longer, said the father. With it, the family accepted that it was time for the daughter to die.

"I WAS SO HAPPY"

Another patient who contacted me (and was not part of the study) told of a predeath vision that happened to her mother. It was an emotionally healing experience for a family that had been wracked by the cancer death of a son only the year before. The woman describes the experience:

"In 1979, our son Tom died of leukemia at the age of ten. About a year later my mother became very ill with cancer and had to be placed in a nursing home. We visited her every day.

"One day when we entered the room, she was talking to someone. She was looking at them as though they were standing right next to her, but we could see no one.

" 'Who are you talking to?' I asked.

" 'I am talking to Tom,' she said.

"Over the course of the next two weeks, my mother had long conversations with Tom as well as with her dead mother and sister. In the hours before she died, she was visited by all three of them. It was a relief for us since they helped her to die, and they helped us to accept her death."

* * *

The woman who told me about this deathbed vision didn't focus on whether the deceased members of her family had really spoken to her mother. Instead, she felt the most important thing was that her mother at least "thought" she was being talked to by family members who had died.

Predeath visions have taught me to listen to patients. I no longer have to be in control all the time. When the patient is dying, I can listen to what the patient is going through. Once we learn to listen again to dying patients, we can develop new ways of helping them through their darkest hour.

Just what *was* I trying to do with my Seattle study? I was just trying to listen. My study wasn't an attempt to prove life after death. It wasn't an attempt to prove reincarnation. It was simply a means of listening to patients and learning from them.

I have found that parents and doctors alike feel responsible for the death of a child. The parents wonder if the illness is something genetic or perhaps the result of their life-style. The physician is concerned that he may not have used the right dose of medication at the right time, as though there is always a right dose of medication.

Frequently, neither party is listening to the patient, who is telling them that he or she is ready to die. I simply felt that the seeds of healing for the living might be found in the visions and perceptions of the dying.

4

Spirit in Medicine

"Ah my good Lord, think you then so soon to die?"

"Yes," replied Gawain. "I tell you that I shall not live two days."

Neither his doctor nor his friends nor his priest knew as much as Gawain about how much time he had left.

—*La Chanson de Roland*

To research near-death experiences today is to be lumped together with spiritualists, TV ministers, and UFOlogists. Medical science ignores the dying process and the fact that it involves presentiments of death and visions. Modern science has developed new medical techniques but not the new rituals to help us deal with the lingering type of death it brings.

Death has now become dirty—a failure—and medicalized. In the hospital, death is no longer the observance of a ritual over which the dying person presides, his friends and relatives gathered around him; rather it is a technical feat achieved when medical treatment is withdrawn. Today, in the great majority of cases, the dying person has already lost consciousness or is heavily sedated. As French historian Philippe Ariès said in a series of lectures on death at Johns Hopkins University, "Death has been dissected, cut to bits by a series of little steps, which finally makes it impossible to know which step was the real death, the one in which consciousness was lost, or the one in which breathing stopped. All of these little silent deaths have replaced and erased the once great dramatic act of death, and no one has the patience or strength to wait over a period of weeks for a moment which has lost its meaning."

It has become difficult to define death. This blurring of the line between life and death has changed how we respond to dying. I have been involved in several cases where, based on brain-wave tracings and medical studies, the courts had to decide whether or not brain-damaged children were dead. Simply being unable to breathe or maintain a heartbeat is not enough to determine if someone is dead anymore. As a cardiologist in my hospital put it: "These days, deciding if a patient has passed on is often a group decision involving the family and the doctors."

Geoffrey Gorer, an authority on death and dying, says that death has replaced sex as the forbidden topic. Today, sex education is part of the schoolchild's curriculum. Death education is ignored. Says Gorer: "One has the right to cry only if no one else can see or hear. Solitary and shameful mourning is the only recourse, like a sort of masturbation."

Research has shown death to be a taboo topic in many hospital situations. Myra Bluebond-Langner, a Rutgers University anthropologist, spent many months as a silent observer on a cancer treatment ward for children. She carefully documented the many subtle ways that doctors, nurses, parents, and even the children themselves create a world of pretense and concealment of the actual diagnosis.

Sociologists Barney Glaser and Anselm Strauss have made observations similar to those of Bluebond-Langner and have even formulated the unwritten rules that physicians, nurses, and dying patients and their parents adhere to in their interactions. According to their research:

- All parties avoid "dangerous" topics: These topics include the child's physical appearance, future events and holidays, future plans outside the hospital, or even what medications the child is being given.
- Discussions of "dangerous" topics stop immediately if someone becomes emotional: Glaser and Strauss found that as soon as the patient, parent, or medical personnel began to cry, the discussion was halted. I have found in my own experience that if I can simply wait for a few minutes until the emotion subsides then some very productive talks can take place. I have also found that the most painful times are those spent telling parents or patient that a course of treatment isn't working.
- When something happens to expose the fiction that is being sustained, then everyone pretends that nothing went awry: For example, in her research Dr. Bluebond-Langner describes a therapist who tells a

child to draw whatever he wants. The child responds by drawing a grave. The therapist immediately took a break from picture drawing.

- All parties strive to keep interaction normal: As death approaches, more effort is spent pretending that everything is normal. The researchers cited above found a dramatic increase in the discussion of such "safe" topics as ward activities, restaurants, movies, television programs, and so forth.
- All parties strive to keep interactions brief: When reality intrudes, all parties strive to end the interaction.

If we doctors and nurses can't discuss holidays with dying patients because they may not be alive for the holiday and we can't even discuss medications that they are taking, how can we feel comfortable discussing predeath visions? Most of us aren't. Yet these visions potentially may give the patient a sense of control and may alleviate the terrible anxiety, fear, depression, anger, and guilt that a child's death can generate in those who take care of him.

THE LOVING LIE

Our current attitudes toward death started developing in the mid-1800s, when physicians began lying to patients about their true prognoses. I call this "the loving lie." Rather than tell a patient that death was imminent and that they should get their affairs in order, physicians instead told the patient that they would soon recover or that a new medical treatment would be started. As recently as ten years ago, most physicians felt that such lying was ethical and in the patient's best interest.

Since the loving lie can only be maintained if the patient is kept ignorant, physicians became less willing to answer questions. Patients ask fewer questions, too. The patient and the physician thus enter into a mutual pact not to discuss death. *Children especially avoid discussing death because they recognize that people visit them less if they ask questions.*

Medical technology makes it hard for physicians to accept death. They have been told a loving lie by the creators of medical technology. They believe that machines can postpone death. This technology—beneficial as it is—has made a terrible parody of death. Instead of a deathbed scene in which the patient shares a last moment with family and friends, people are more likely to be surrounded and sustained by machines. They may not even have the benefit of priest, minister, or physician. A dying person is likely to be unconscious and completely out of control.

When a patient dies, the situation becomes quite different. The hospital erupts into a spasm of frenzied activity. Dozens of people rush to the bedside in a last-ditch effort to resuscitate the patient. The essentially dead patient is pumped full of drugs, stabbed with dozens of needles, and jolted with electric shocks. Our dying moments are closely documented by heart rate, levels of oxygen in the blood, brain wave readings, and so forth. Finally, when the last doctor has had enough, this technohysteria comes to an end.

I have participated in many such scenes, and I know
that nobody really knows when to stop. Many times
with Airlift Northwest we would pick up children who
had no chance of surviving and aggressively resuscitate them for the two or three hours it took to get them
to Children's Hospital, where they would die in the
intensive care unit.

For example, a child was found submerged for over
an hour in an open septic tank. This child was aggressively resuscitated even though we all knew that,
even if the heart and lungs were revitalized, there
would be no chance that the brain would survive.

We did this because of the loving lie. We are unable
to say simply, "Your child is going to die, and nothing
can be done to prevent it." We wanted the parent to
believe that everything possible was being done. Unfortunately, "doing everything" often meant taking
dying children for a five-hundred-mile airplane ride
only to have them die alone, separated from their parents.

I am not criticizing the airlift program, which is run
by the most conscientious and professional doctors and
nurses with whom I have ever worked. And indeed,
we were responsible for several miraculous recoveries
in which patients were revived and lived happily when
we all felt that, if we managed to keep them alive,
they would probably be brain damaged. I am only
sharing our secret thoughts about death, and the sad
fact that we are both helped and blinded by technology.

BLINDED BY SCIENCE

How blinded are we? A Swiss study gives a glaring example of how the comforting aspects of predeath visions can be ignored.

This study scientifically documents that the parents of children who die of crib death often have premonitions of that event. It is an important study because it illustrates the psychic connection that mothers have always believed existed between them and their children. The researchers conclude something quite different.

The study acknowledges that the parents have premonitions of their children's death. The researchers then make an astonishing leap and conclude that the parents have a deep-seated wish for their children to die. They speculate that this leads to an emotional neglect that the child senses and that then causes its death.

The irony is that these researchers could have brought great comfort to the parents of crib-death victims by demonstrating to them that predeath visions are a normal and natural part of the dying process. Instead, their scientific materialism does not accept the existence of predeath visions. They had already dismissed predeath experiences as a reality, so they reach what they think is a scientifically logical conclusion: The parents must have wished their babies to death.

How can I share such "scientific" conclusions as these with a patient I'll call Mary Anderson? She had been a pediatric nurse for fifteen years and was as level-headed as one would expect in that profession.

On her wedding night, she had a very vivid dream that their first child would die. The next morning she shared that frightening dream with her husband.

About six months before her newborn child died, she had a premonition that her child would die of crib death. This time she told a seven-year-old boy in the neighborhood who had suffered the unexpected loss of his father. She confided to him that she too would soon suffer such a loss.

She had strong feelings that the end was near the day before her baby died. She took many pictures of the child and cried all night.

She was able to cope with her baby's death only because her church leader interpreted the premonitions as meaning that the child was called to heaven by God. His gentle message incorporated grief and acceptance. Its healing effects far exceeded the truckload of grief that would have been dumped on Mary had I told her there was "scientific proof" that the death was her fault.

I have a premonition of my own to contribute here. Months before my father died, he sat down in my living room and told me that he was going to die soon.

Most of my father's intestines had been surgically removed ten years earlier for cancer of the colon, and he had had triple bypass surgery. On top of that he refused to take his heart medicine since it left him impotent.

My dad was headstrong, so I wasn't really surprised

by his decision. As a physician, I did make sure he knew all the ramifications of not taking his medicine; as his son, I knew that arguing with him was meaningless—he was going to do whatever he wanted.

The night he died, I was exhausted from work and had turned off my telephone. As I dozed off, I saw my father. "Melvin, call your answering service," he said. "I have something to tell you." I called and was told to contact my mother immediately. She told me that he had died.

I learned from my own encounter that death has natural and supernatural signs. As a physician, I saw the signs of death in my father from his breathing patterns, the way he talked, and his coloring. I had a vision the night he died, perhaps triggered by my unconscious understanding of how ill he had been during his last visit, three months before. I don't want these supernatural signs to be "scientifically" explained (or explained away) to me. I doubt that they can be. I do want them to be accepted by my peers. These things happen and don't need to be explained away.

C. G. Jung described a supernatural dream in his book, *Memories, Dreams, Reflections.*

"One night I lay awake thinking of the sudden death of a friend whose funeral had taken place the day before. I was deeply concerned. Suddenly I felt that he was in the room. It seemed to me that he stood at the foot of my bed and was asking me to go with him. I did not have the feeling of an apparition; rather, it was an inner visual image of him, which I explained to myself as a fantasy. But in all honesty I had to ask myself, 'Do I have any proof that this is a fantasy? Suppose it is not a fantasy, suppose my friend is really here and I decided he was only a fantasy—would that not be abominable of me?' Yet I had equally little proof that he stood before me as an apparition. Then I said to myself, 'Proof is neither here nor there! Instead of explaining him away as a fantasy, I might just as well give him the benefit of the doubt and for experiment's sake credit him with reality.' The moment I had that thought, he went to the door and beckoned me to follow him. So I was going to have to play along with him! That was something I hadn't bargained for. I had to repeat my argument to myself once more. Only then did I follow him in my imagination.

"He led me out of the house, into the garden, out to the road, and finally to his house. (In reality it was several hundred yards away from mine.) I went in, and he conducted me into his study. He climbed on a stool and showed me the second of five books with red bindings which stood on the second shelf from the top. Then the vision broke off. I was not acquainted with his library and did not know what books he owned. Certainly I could never have made out from below the titles of the books he had pointed out to me on the second shelf from the top.

"This experience seemed to me so curious that next morning I went to his widow and asked whether I could look up something in my friend's library. Sure enough, there was a stool standing under the bookcase I had seen in my vision, and even before I came closer I could see five books with red bindings. I stepped up on the stool so as to be able to read the titles. They were translations of the novels of Emile Zola. The title of the second volume read:

'The Legacy of the Dead.' The contents seemed to me of no interest. Only the title was extremely significant in connection with this experience."

The lesson to be learned from this type of dream experience, said Jung, is to have no preconceived opinions about "the statements made by dreams." Jung conceded that there is really no way to prove life after death. But such events as predeath visions, near-death experiences, and apparitions are hints that something survives death.

WHEN "SUPERNATURAL" WAS NATURAL

There was a time when presentiments of death were widely known, discussed, and even expected. Near-death experiences were not considered paranormal or supernatural. I think they should be treated that way again. They are natural signs of death, along with pre-death visions and near-death experiences. Science has not disproven the validity of these visions; rather it has simply ignored them. The near-death experiences of children remind us of forgotten ancient truths. This wisdom from the mouths of babes can teach us new and healthier ways of understanding our own deaths.

I am sad that I never shared my vision about my father with my family or discussed with them the feelings my father shared with me before he died. It might have helped us cope with the terrible guilt and unresolved emotion that a parent's death can generate. What kept me from sharing these feelings was the attitude of my profession built by years of medical training.

Death is an integral part of life. We all must face death as part of the price of living. We have replaced the deathbed scene with the loving lie, in which both physician and patient deny the reality of the situation. French philosopher Pere de Dainville said, as he lay dying in an intensive care unit with tubes protruding from every orifice of his body, "They are cheating me out of my own death."

CONJURED DEATHS AND ANCIENT RULERS

Deep in an underground chamber a solemn group of men is seeking guidance from death. They are dressed in white robes and chanting softly around a casket that is sealed with wax. One of their members is steadfastly counting to himself, carefully marking the time. After about eight minutes, the casket is opened, and the man who nearly suffocated inside is revived by the rush of fresh air. He tells the men around him what he saw. As he passed out from lack of oxygen, he saw a light that became brighter and larger as he sped toward it through a tunnel. From that light came a radiant person in white who delivered a message of eternal life.

The priest who is attending this ceremony is pleased with the results. "No man escapes death," he says. "And every living soul is destined to resurrection. You go into the tomb alive that you will learn of the light."

The man who "died" but is now reborn is happy. He is now a member of one of the strangest societies in history, a group of civic leaders who induced nearly fatal suffocation to create a near-death experience.

Sound like a cult from some place in northern California? ex-hippies looking for a new high, perhaps? Not at all. This was the cult of Osiris, a small society of men who were the priests and pharaohs of ancient Egypt, one of the greatest civilizations in human history. This account of how they inspired near death is an actual description of their rites from Egyptologists who have translated their hieroglyphics.

One of the most important Egyptian rituals involved the reenactment by their god-king of the myth of Osiris, the god who brought agriculture and civilization to the ancient Egyptians. He was the first king of Egypt who civilized his subjects and then traveled abroad to instruct others in the fine art of civilization. His enemies plotted against him. Upon his return to Egypt, he was captured and sealed in a chest. His eventual resurrection was seen as proof of life eternal.

Each new king was supposed to be a direct reincarnation of Osiris. An important part of the ceremony was to reenact his entombment. These rituals took place in the depths of the Great Pyramid and were a prerequisite for becoming a god-king. It is my guess that many slaves perished while the Egyptians experimented to find exactly how long a person could be sealed in an airtight container and survive.

Nonetheless, these near-death experiences were more important to the Egyptians than the lives of a few slaves. After all, this was the age of the bicameral mind, a period in which men believed that their thoughts came to them from the gods and were not internally generated. For the Egyptians, thoughts and dreams were gods speaking to them.

Prior to the evolution of individual consciousness, people were what Princeton psychiatrist Julian Jaynes calls "bicameral." By this, he means that they did not understand that their own thoughts and actions were generated from within themselves, but rather that they thought external gods created these thoughts and actions. For example, a fully conscious human thinks: I am hungry and I will make myself a sandwich. The bicameral man thought: The gods have created a pain in my belly and cause me to find food to satisfy them. *The Iliad* is an excellent example of bicameral thinking: It is one god who makes Achilles promise not to go into battle, another who urges him to go, and another screams through his throat (at his enemies). In fact, the gods take the place of consciousness. The beginnings of action are not in conscious plans, reasons, and motives; they are—to the bicameral man— the actions and speeches of gods.

This bicameral thinking has long vanished from human beings, ever since the evolution of language and writing. Once men could write down their thoughts, and read what other people have written, they came to understand that each human being has an individual consciousness, and that gods do not direct our every action.

However, ancient Egypt was a prime example of a

bicameral society. Jaynes states that Egyptian civilization was controlled and directed by the bicameral voice of their first god-king, Osiris. It was essential to their civilization that each new king consider himself to be the vehicle of the hallucinated voice of the dead king whose admonitions still controlled society. What better way to generate this absolute continuity of the god-king than to have each new king undergo a near-death experience. Just as children that I interviewed often perceived the light that they saw as the light of Jesus, these king-initiates would perceive that same light as the spirit of Osiris.

A near-death experience to a bicameral man would have extraordinary significance, more so even than it has to modern man. For one thing, it would be absolute proof of eternal life. Since they felt that the gods inspired their every thought, a near-death experience would be like having a god open the doors of perception to a mortal.

An NDE gave Egyptian rulers a sense of all-knowing. Before they were sealed into the casket, they only acted like kings. Afterward, they felt as if they had deeper knowledge of the world around them.

I also believe that an NDE as part of a king's job description may account for the unusual peace and prosperity that Egypt enjoyed for the nearly two thousand years that the pharaohs reigned. As happens with those who experience NDEs today, these kings were transformed by the humbling and exalting experience of near death. They developed a reverence for the love that people share with one another. They became kind and caring and interested in the universe and the world around them.

These were people who supported extensive research in astronomy. With their "primitive" tools, they were able to obtain a vast knowledge of the stars, even finding dark stars that we have been able to confirm only with powerful telescopes.

The ancient Egyptians were advanced in medicine and the use of foods and antibiotics to prevent epidemics among pyramid workers. They knew of special diets of red onions, bread, and garlic that stimulated the immune system, a diet that was only recently endorsed by the National Science Foundation. They even had a fair amount of knowledge about surgery.

Archaeologists have deciphered the exact experience of these mystery rituals, and virtually all agree that its purpose was to generate an understanding of eternal life. Their understanding of the death process has been handed down through the ages in a document known as *The Egyptian Book of the Dead*. This book is simply a detailed description of a near-death experience. It starts with a judgment scene and goes on to reveal many gods and various voices, continues on a long boat trip through a dark tunnel, and ends with union with a bright light.

The Egyptian Book of the Dead is quite similar to *The Tibetan Book of the Dead*, a manual for dying that was passed by word of mouth in Tibetan culture until about fifteen hundred years ago, when it was recorded by Europeans.

The Tibetan Book of the Dead gives the dying person control over his own death and rebirth. The Tibetans, who believed in reincarnation, felt that the dying person could influence his own destiny. The Tibetans called this book *Bardo Thödol*, or "Liberation by Hearing on the After-Death Plane." It was meant to be read *after* death to help the deceased find the right path.

Part of what the priest is supposed to read goes like this: "Thy own intellect, which is now voidness . . . thine own consciousness, not formed into anything, in reality void . . . will first experience the Radiance of the Fundamental Clear Light of Pure Reality.

"The union of your own consciousness and the Clear Light is the state of Perfect Enlightenment. This is the Great Body of Clear Light . . . the source of life and light."

How similar the Tibetan beliefs to the Egyptians and other ancient people too, from Europe to Africa.

The Aztec Song of the Dead represents a work that served to enlighten the Aztecs about the world beyond. This was a society that practiced ritual and slow death as part of their basic religion.

Their *Song of the Dead* tells the story of Quetzalcoatl, their god and legendary king who discovered the arts, science, and agriculture and who represented the forces of civilization, good and light. He is described by his people as "igniting the creations of man's hands and the imagination of his heart."

Their *Song of the Dead* reads like a poetic version of a near-death experience. It practically scores off the top of the scale of the Near-Death Experience Validity

Scale developed by researcher Kenneth Ring. The *Song* reads like this:

"Then the time came for Quetzalcoatl to die, when he felt the darkness twist in him like a river."

He then had a life review, in which he remembers all of his good works and is able to settle his affairs. He then "saw my face/(like looking into a) cracked mirror." He hears flutes and the voices of friends and then passes through a shining city and over hills of many colors. He comes to the edge of a great sea, where he again sees his own face, during which time "the beauty of his face returned to him."

There is a bonfire on the beach in which he throws himself, and . . .

It ended with his heart transformed into a star.

It ended with the morning star with dawn and evening.

It ended with his journey to Death's kingdom with seven days of darkness.

With his body changed to light.

A star that burns forever in that sky.

All of these cultures believed they left their bodies and embarked on a spiritual voyage, a journey that had the same traits as that of Katie, who nearly drowned in that swimming pool in Idaho.

SCIENCE: THE NEW RELIGION

Virtually all primitive societies—not just the relatively recent Egyptian and Tibetan—believed in survival after death.

In fact, it has only been in the last two hundred years (and then primarily in Western civilization) that the belief in a hereafter has been abandoned as "unscientific." Science is our religion now. Genetic engineering and heart transplants are our hope of eternal life. Life after death is seen as a subject that is unworthy of scientific investigation. When science turns its spotlight on life after death, it is usually trying to debunk it.

How is it that we have forgotten the knowledge of the ancients? What transpired so that these cosmic truths taken for granted by our ancestors are now largely forgotten or ridiculed? How is it that many physicians have stopped observing and listening?

Only twenty years ago, it came as a complete surprise to the medical profession that dying people actually went through a variety of psychological stages before passing on. In her hotly debated "pioneering" work, *On Death and Dying*, Elisabeth Kübler-Ross claimed that there were five stages of dying: denial, anger, bargaining, depression, and acceptance. Yet this "hotly debated" information has long been common knowledge to most nurses, who attend patients and talk to them instead of at them.

The medical establishment has managed to make near-death experiences a freakish event, not the rule. It has convinced patients that they are having bad dreams, not profound experiences that bond them with all of humanity.

As a medical doctor and someone who has been privileged to hear hundreds of childhood NDEs, I became intensely interested in why we no longer believe in life after death. Why do so many of my colleagues react negatively to this subject? Why does the medical establishment assume that NDEs are hallucinations?

What has changed in Western society that has led to this massive denial of death? By the time our children reach adulthood, they have seen over a thousand violent deaths on television, yet they have no concept of what is involved in the dying process.

How have we gotten ourselves into this situation?

THE SCIENTIFIC REVOLUTION

Some theologians feel that the change in Western spirituality started in the seventeenth and eighteenth centuries with scientist-philosophers Isaac Newton, John Locke, and John Ray. These three English Protestants and amateur theologians built the foundations of modern science by trying to discover the works of God in the design of the universe. Hence, when the apple bopped Newton on the head, it led to the theory of gravity, the way in which God worked to keep everything on the earth.

Their work, which led to the scientific revolution, was initially an attempt to find the hidden divinity of God within nature. By uncovering the natural laws that controlled the universe, this trio of geniuses believed we could better understand God.

These scientists were deeply religious. Newton, for example, was more proud of his treatise on the Book of Daniel than of being the father of physics. However, studying nature to find the laws of God proved to be a slippery enterprise. The Catholic Church, which never really recovered from its attempt to suppress Galileo's theory that the earth rotated around the sun, was powerless to stop the development of scientific thought. Rather than welcome it as an acceptable addendum to religion, the church fought it. Since that time, religion has found itself squarely opposite science.

The study of nature was abandoned to the scientists, with religious leaders focusing on the immortal soul and metaphysics while at the same time claiming that some scientific discoveries were "the devil's work." Darwin's theory of evolution and the subsequent fossil evidence supporting his theory conflicted with the theologian's account of creation. Advances in obstetrics, including the use of anesthesia, were bitterly reviled by the clergy, who claimed that "man should be born in pain."

A greater schism developed between church and science. Religion basically yielded nature to science and became master of the metaphysical world, which could be entered only by following the word of God—as they read it.

The triumph of science in interpreting the world weakened the role of the church. By the late 1800s, many people no longer believed in heaven and hell. Church attendance dropped dramatically as the Industrial Revolution rapidly vindicated science as the new God.

This period also marked the birth of medical materialism. Science became almost numbed with excitement at the dramatic discoveries. Physicians discovered that germs caused many diseases, a finding that ultimately led to antibiotics. The effects of nutrition on disease were discovered. Surgeons were learning how to control infections.

Where early physicians had always incorporated religion into their healing practices, they now omitted it. Having been forced to choose between theology and science, they went with science. What else could they do? Most religions had rejected the importance of the body in favor of the healthy soul. The possibility that religion and science could peacefully coexist was not an option.

This lopsided view continues to this day. Now surgeons are able to remove appendices, replace hip joints, and even transplant hearts. As science progresses, we are able to manipulate nature through genetic engineering.

As quickly as science has advanced toward unlocking nature's secrets, we have moved away from spirituality and the possibility of a life beyond. After all, it is an intangible subject as far as science is concerned. Is there a way to conduct an experiment proving the afterlife that yields reproducable results? No. Is there anything for a scientist other than anecdotal or scriptural evidence? Not so far.

So what's the point? ask modern scientists. Call near-death experiences "hallucinations," and let's get on with "legitimate" research.

With the explosion of scientific knowledge, we have

seen a brutal revolution in traditional ideas and feelings. Less than a hundred years ago, most people died at home, surrounded by a multigenerational family and loved ones. Today, most people die alone in hospitals. Today, fewer than half of American households are composed of two biological parents and children. Fewer still include grandparents.

THE INVISIBLE DEATH

The growth of medical technology and the loss of religious involvement in the healing or dying process have greatly changed our attitudes about death. The focus is on the living and the losses they will incur. It is widely assumed that those who are near death are beyond knowing.

Deathbed rituals have been abandoned. Predeath visions have been forgotten or discarded as hallucinations. The loving lie shields everyone against the inevitable. Medical science—with its ability to use machines in place of failed organs—has replaced religion as the key to immortality.

The attitude of society toward death has changed. Today we ignore death.

A portion of an article on California sums up our national attitude on the subject: "Death is simply not a component of what passes, out here, for the seasonal cycle. You cruise along the freeway in sunshine and shirtsleeves, and then one day it rains, and you realize that for two weeks it's been February. As a result, people don't really 'get' death out here, which means they don't get the kind of grown-up seriousness that mortality inspires. Not that people don't drop dead, of course. But the deaths of others are seen as aberrations, a violation of the L.A. ethic. 'Everything's so nice here,' is the unspoken attitude. 'You'd have to be crazy to die.' '' Such is the attitude of many about death.

JOINING SCIENCE AND SPIRIT

All things considered, one can see why gaining acceptance for researching near-death experiences is so difficult. Not only are researchers out of the realm of medical science, but theologians generally don't trust scientists who wander into their field. Combine these factors with Western civilization's phobia about death and it is obvious why NDE researchers are firmly planted in no-man's land.

It is a risk to reputation and profession to conduct near-death research these days. The handful of people who do it accept that risk. Why? For me the answer is simple: NDEs are the way to join science and spiritualism.

Attitudes are already changing toward the effect the mind can have on the body. It is part of that grand lesson we were taught in medical school, ''Treat the whole patient; don't just treat the disease.''

Let me give you some examples of the mind's effect upon the body, well-researched statements of fact that would have been heresy a few years ago.

* * *

Children Treated for Mother's Disorders: A series of studies asked mothers to keep diaries about their lives. These diaries were later analyzed for evidence of mental stress. It was shown that at times of increased stress, mothers took their kids to doctors for colds and earaches. The child's illness was a response to the stress they felt from their mothers and proof of a dynamic between mother and child.

Envisioning Health: Solid research has shown that self-hypnosis and visualization are powerful tools in the fight against illness.

For instance, when children with leukemia are taught to visualize their cancer cells being eaten by hungry fish, their survival time increases.

Also, children being treated with chemotherapy can use self-hypnosis to stop severe vomiting.

Biofeedback and the use of imagery have been shown to be more effective than medication in controlling migraines in children.

Imagining Makes It So: Even cosmetic surgery can be accomplished to some extent by the mind. Many excellent studies have shown that self-hypnosis can typically add two inches to a woman's bustline! Yet few physicians refer a woman wanting larger breasts to a hypnotist.

This research and much more like it reveal the mind's effect on such illnesses as heart disease and cancer, even disorders like warts and shingles, which often can be eliminated by hypnotherapy. It proves that the door is opening in medical science and the mind is creeping in.

Medical science is starting to accept that it has something important to learn from the near-death experiences of children. If nothing more, they have grudgingly admitted that comatose patients, who seem to be in the last stages of life, may actually be undergoing a profound experience that involves total awareness of what is going on around them. By studying near-death experiences and incorporating that knowledge into our medical system, we can take the giant step toward respecting the death and dying that are part of our daily medical practice.

Does this mean we have to believe in the existence of a soul? Does it mean we have to believe that we are reincarnated? Not at all. It means that we need to acknowledge the healing power of a near-death experience. Let me give an example of what I mean.

A pediatric anesthesiologist told me that he witnessed a near-death experience that changed his entire approach to medicine and made him far more sensitive to the inner needs of patients.

While chief resident at a children's hospital in Little Rock, Arkansas, this doctor was called upon to resuscitate a seven-year-old boy who'd had a near-fatal reaction to intensive chemotherapy for leukemia.

When he shocked the boy with cardioversion paddles to restart his heart, the boy's eyes sprung open and flashed with anger.

Several weeks later, when this doctor was making rounds late at night, he was called by the boy as he passed his room. "Doctor, where is Jesus?"

The doctor didn't know what to say. "He's everywhere," he finally said.

"That's not what I mean," said the boy. "What did you do to make Jesus go away? Jesus and I were above you watching you put a tube into my throat. Then you shocked me with that machine, and you made Jesus go away. Why did you do that? I'm mad at you for making him go away."

"We were trying to help you," said the doctor.

"I know that," said the boy. "But I was all right with Jesus, and I didn't want to come back. Jesus was taking care of me."

The doctor dismissed the experience from his mind. It wasn't until a few years later that he read of my patients in a medical journal and contacted me. He told me about the young boy's near-death experience and said he wished he would have known about NDEs earlier. "It would have comforted the parents to know that their son felt safe with Jesus."

Some debunkers are so preoccupied with proving that NDEs are not proof of an afterlife that they overlook the fact that they teach us important things about the way we live and die. As this doctor told me: "Michael thought he was safe with Jesus and that was good enough for him. What I believed didn't matter."

TIME FOR CHANGE

I think it is time to change the way we deal with critically ill patients.

For instance, intensive care units should be designed so that visitors will be welcome and won't be in the way of the many machines and medical procedures that are absolutely necessary. It is also important to talk positively and frequently to the comatose or dying patients since we now know that they may be much more aware of things around them than we realize. Indeed, they may even be hovering above us as we administer to them!

Make the patient's spiritual needs a routine part of daily rounds, just as much a part of his medical chart as a detailed description of urine output.

It isn't important for the medical establishment to accept near-death experiences as proof of a life beyond this one. It is important that they not dismiss them as deathbed fantasies or categorize them as bad dreams. They are real to the person who has them and should be used accordingly as a healing tool.

These experiences can be used to inspire faith. As the great physician Sir William Osler said: "Nothing in life is more wonderful than faith—the one great moving force which we can never weigh in the balance nor test in the laboratory."

MEDICINE + SPIRIT

Let me give you an example of medicine and faith working together. I don't quite know what to make of this story, which was told to me by a doctor who witnessed it from beginning to end in the small Idaho hospital where it happened.

A woman was having severe complications during the delivery of her child. Not only was the placenta separating from the lining of the uterus (a pediatric emergency), but the obtuse angle of the child's head in the birth canal was making delivery very difficult. When the child was finally delivered, he was found to have a severe brain hemorrhage.

The child spent several months in the intensive care unit of this small town because the mother did not want to transfer him to a large city where she would not be allowed to spend full time with him. Doctors decided not to encourage her to move the child since they felt the injuries were so massive that no treatment would be possible.

The child had severe cerebral palsy secondary to brain damage and a seizure disorder that had shown up on an abnormal EEG. These are afflictions from which children simply don't recover. If they survive infancy, they spend their lives severely retarded.

The doctors told her their prognosis, but still the mother stayed with her child. By all accounts she was with the boy almost twenty-four hours a day for several months. Perhaps it was the strain of the ordeal or sleep deprivation that led to what happened next.

Late one night, she said, a Being of Light came into her hospital room. Later she described it as having the shape of a person, but not the features of either a male or a female. It glowed with a cold, gray light as though light were being beamed through an ice cube.

"Your son will be all right," the being said.

The woman said that she felt as though love were being poured into her body. "It was marvelous."

The next day she shared this vision with her medical team. She was especially excited because the being had assured her that her son was going to be normal. Could they please do another EEG to see if anything had happened?

They repeated the brain-wave test and came up with the startling results: normal. The child had made a full recovery.

HEALING THE SPLIT

I was deeply moved by this mother's story. I feel that just understanding near-death experiences will be our first step at healing the great division between science and religion that started with Isaac Newton almost three hundred years ago. Educating physicians, nurses, and ourselves about what people experience in those final hours will shatter our prejudices about the ways we think about medicine and life.

Such understanding will not return us to the outdated religions and rituals that did not keep pace with modern science. We will combine the essence of those ancient truths with scientific knowledge and create new rituals with which to heal our inner selves and society.

5

The Seat of the Soul Hypothesis

Everyone now knows how to find the meaning of life
within himself. But less than a century ago, men and
women did not have access to the puzzle boxes within
themselves. They could not name even one of the 53
portals to the soul.

—*Kurt Vonnegut*, The Sirens of Titan

A twenty-eight-year-old patient told me a sad but wonderful tale about her near-death experience as a child.
Her family told me the rest later, including premonitions of her own death.

June had had a cardiac arrest at the age of five during surgery to repair her heart valves and to install a
pacemaker. She often talked about her near-death experience, mainly because it was such a beautiful event
that it always seemed to be with her.

Although she was deeply anesthetized during the
surgery, she suddenly found herself floating above the

doctors, watching them as they worked. She could re-count details: the appearance of certain instruments, for instance, and the fact that one of the doctors was right-handed and the other left-handed.

When the doctors began their procedure to restart her heart, she found herself leaving the operating room and traveling down a long tunnel. At the other end, she was bathed in light, a bright warm light that she always described as "the Light of God." As she told her husband, Don, "I was never afraid again after I experienced the light. I know that I can die at any time, and yet I have no fear."

It was the experience of this light that gave her such a positive outlook on life. Without it, much of her life would have been dark. Her parents died when she was young. Her sister died of a drug overdose at the age of eighteen.

June knew that pacemakers sometimes stop work-ing, causing heart failure, but she didn't dwell on it. "I was more afraid than she was," said Don. "She had no fear because she had seen the light."

The day before she died June was having a cup of coffee at her kitchen table, when her dead sister ap-peared. She stood before her and announced, "June, it's time to go." Then the apparition sat down across the table and drank a cup of coffee. When the ap-parition finished, she simply got up and left the house.

June felt that she couldn't tell her husband what had happened. Instead, she called the aunt and uncle who had raised her and told them about the peculiar occurrence. "I am going to die, and I just wanted to say good-bye," she said. Then she called her two brothers. She told them not to mention their conversation to her husband until she died because it would be too upsetting for him.

She simply told Don how happy he had made her. She was glad to have such a beautiful home and a wonderful child. Nothing could have made her happier.

That night she died in her sleep because her pacemaker failed. Her heart simply stopped.

Story after story, puzzle after puzzle, case studies like this one come along.

Do these mysterious tales prove the existence of a higher plane? Do they prove the existence of the soul, a part of us that leaves the body, flies up that tunnel, and, well, goes to heaven?

Science has long debunked the spirit because of its intangibility. For the past hundred years, neuroscience has concentrated on exploring the intricate connections between brain and body that allow us to walk, breathe, and use the senses of hearing, seeing, touching, tasting, and smelling. Most neurologists are not interested in studying consciousness. Denying the existence of the soul, scientists define the brain as limited to neuron and electrochemical reactions that cause observable behavior. To admit to more would be to confess that there is more to the human mind than simply the brain.

PHILOSOPHY OF THE SOUL

The soul has been widely defined throughout history. Some societies have believed that the soul represents the highest of human thought, and therefore, it is most abstract and difficult to define. Others have believed that the soul represents the source of life itself, while others have considered the soul only to be the source of afterlife.

Democritus, a fifth-century Greek philosopher, felt that life was sustained by "psychic atoms" that were spread throughout the body but were controlled by the brain, which contained "the bonds of the soul." Plato theorized that the soul had three parts—intellectual, irascible, and sexual—but only the first aspect had the virtue of immortality.

Galen, the first-century Greek physician, agreed with Plato, but went further. He divided the soul into several functions. All of our motor and sensory abilities were attributed to the soul as were "rational" functions such as imagination, reason, and memory.

The Catholic Church appropriated and developed Galen's concept of the soul, even offering opinions as to where the various functions were located in the brain. There the issue rested for almost fifteen hundred years, researchers and philosophers keeping their opinions to themselves regarding the soul lest they offend the doctrines of the church.

French philosopher René Descartes offered the viewpoint that is dominant in the Western world today. He felt that the body was a machine composed of bones, blood, muscles, nerves, and skin and controlled by the brain. The soul, according to Descartes, was something only found in human beings and not in animals. It couldn't be divided into parts the way Plato said it could. It was unique, immaterial, and immortal. This theory was called dualism.

Many accepted the dualism of Descartes then, and many still accept it today. Many accept only half of the dualistic argument, the half that says the body is a machine.

Scientists who fit into that category are known as "behaviorists," researchers who believe that all human and animal functions can be explained by observable behaviors. For the most part, they see man as nothing more than a complex animal or machine. Indeed, throughout history many have sought to create an artificial man. About a century after Descartes, Jacques de Vaucanson, a builder of automatons, and a French physician named Claude LeCat even went so far as to make a duck that could flap its wings and digest seeds. The soul was not discussed by those who studied the brain and the body because it could not be observed. French physician Julien Offray de la Mettrie even put forth the notion in the eighteenth century that the soul could easily be removed in most men without losing much of the man himself—if they could find the soul, that is.

The invention of the computer seemed further to vindicate the behavioral approach. Throughout the 1950s and 1960s, most brain scientists considered philosophy to be "silly" and unrelated to the real work of discovering the circuitry of the brain. The self-conscious philosopher, rather than attempting to understand the soul as philosophers had since the days of Plato, took up the question of whether computers would ever be able to think or have emotions.

To a great extent, this type of thinking persists today. Richard Restak, the acclaimed neurologist who wrote a book entitled *The Brain*, states that there is no "seat of the mind" and that the entire concept of mind or soul is a philosophical fallacy, nothing more than a literary device. Restak even goes so far as to state that he attempted to find the soul in the brain by using a very sophisticated imaging machine known as a PET scanner. Since he doubted that he could photograph the soul with this machine, he concluded that it must not exist. That was his method of "proving" his hypothesis that man is a soulless creature, at least according to the PET scanner.

I must hasten to add that many researchers in the medical profession feel, deep down in their hearts, that there is a soul. I remember one of my professors at Johns Hopkins University telling me that "When I say, 'I went for a walk today,' I know I am simply describing to you a behavior that my fellow scientists can quantify. But I know that there was more to my walk than just my legs moving. I know that some inner force decided to go for a walk and that that same inner force enjoyed the flowers and birds and the beauty of nature; thoughts that science will never be able to measure or quantify." That statement came from a rigid behaviorist with whom I spent hundreds of hours quantifying the exact frequencies of sounds that monkeys can hear.

When I reflect on what he said, I remember the works of Wilder Penfield.

THE FATHER OF NEUROSCIENCE

Wilder Penfield is widely recognized as the father of neurosurgery. Educated at Princeton, Oxford, and Johns Hopkins, he is responsible for much of our current understanding of brain function.

Among other things, Penfield did extensive "mapping" of the brain in the 1930s and 1940s. To do this, he electrically stimulated various areas of patients' brains during neurosurgery. He was able to do this with the patients under local anesthetic because the brain only perceives pain from the rest of the body and has no ability to feel pain itself. During the procedures, with the patients fully conscious and alert, he would prod different areas electrically and carefully document what happened.

For example, electrical stimulation of the motor cortex would result in movement of the arms or legs. Other areas were documented as being responsible for speech, hearing, vision, and so forth.

Penfield, like many of his medical cohorts, thought for many years that there was no soul or independent consciousness in human beings. He believed that the neurons of the brain could explain all human behavior. Basically, what you see is what you get—three pounds of gelatinous neurons wrapped in a bony skull, the same "soulless" stuff Restak saw on his PET scanner.

At his farm in rural Canada, Penfield used a large rock to illustrate this belief. On one side of the rock, he painted the Greek word for "spirit." On the other side, he drew the outline of a human head with a question mark where the brain should be. He connected the two figures with a solid line linked to the Aesculapian torch, representing medical science. To him, this image meant that questions about the existence of the soul had been answered by science. As far as Penfield was concerned, brain studies could ultimately explain everything about the mind and body.

Fifty years later and in frail health, Penfield changed his mind. He put on six sweaters to keep out the bitter Canadian winter and trudged out to the rock that he had painted with such assurance so many decades earlier. With fresh paint, he crossed out the solid line between the brain and the spirit, replacing it with a dotted line and a question mark. It became a visual reminder that all of his work with the brain had still left many unanswered questions about the mind and the soul. As he said in his last work, *The Mystery of the Mind*, "I came to take seriously, even to believe, that the consciousness of man, the mind, is NOT something to be reduced to brain mechanism."

Penfield went on to say that determining the connection between mind and brain is "the ultimate of ultimate problems."

After years of observing human brains in conscious patients—which went beyond the work of his peers who arrived at their conclusions through psychotherapy or by examining brains of experimental animals—Penfield believed that something differentiated the *mind* from the physical *brain*. As he wrote:

"Taken either way, the nature of the mind presents the fundamental problem, perhaps the most difficult and most important of all problems. For myself, after a professional lifetime spent in trying to discover how the brain accounts for the mind, it comes as a surprise now to discover, during this final examination of the evidence, that the dualist hypothesis (the mind is separate from the brain) seems the more reasonable of explanations.

"Since every man must adopt for himself, without the help of science, his way of life and his personal religion, I have long had my own private beliefs. What a thrill it is, then, to discover that the scientist, too, can legitimately believe in the existence of the spirit!

"Possibly the scientist and the physician could add something by stepping outside the laboratory and the consulting room to reconsider these strangely gifted human beings about us. Where did the mind—call it the spirit if you like—come from? Who can say? It exists. The mind is attached to the action of a certain mechanism within the brain. A mind has been thus attached in the case of every human being for many thousands of generations, and there seems to be significant evidence of heredity in the mind's character from one generation to the next and the next. But at present, one can only say simply and without explanation, 'the mind is born.' "

Pondering the ultimate of ultimate questions, this physician-philosopher asked himself the question: "What becomes of the mind after death?"

"That question brings up the other question so often asked: 'Can the mind communicate directly with other minds?' As far as any clearly proven scientific conclusion goes, the answer to the second question is 'no.' The mind can communicate only through its brain-mechanisms. Certainly it does so most often through the mechanism of speech. Nonetheless, since the exact nature of the mind is a mystery and the source of its energy has yet to be identified, no scientist is in a position to say that direct communication between one active mind and another cannot occur during life. He may say that unassailable evidence of it has not yet been brought forward.

"Direct communications between the mind of man and the mind of God is quite another matter. The argument in favor of this lies in the claim made by so many men for so long a time that they have received guidance and revelation from some power beyond themselves through the medium of prayer. I see no reason to doubt this evidence, nor any means of submitting it to scientific proof.

"Indeed, no scientist, by virtue of his science, has the right to pass judgement on the faiths by which men live and die. We can only set out the data about the brain, and present the physiological hypotheses that are relevant to what the mind does.

"Now we must return, however reluctantly, to the first question: When death at last blows out the candle that was life, the mind seems to vanish, as in sleep. I said 'seems.' What can one really conclude? What is the reasonable hypothesis in regard to this matter, considering the physiological evidence? Only this: the brain has not explained the mind fully.''

After fifty years of studying the living brain, Wilder Penfield realized that the answer to the question, "Is there a soul," was more elusive than ever.

Perhaps the soul does not appear on the latest machine invented by man to study the brain. I believe that by looking carefully at the work of neuroscientists one can conclude that there is, within the human brain, an area that is genetically coded for out-of-body experiences, tunnel experiences, and much of what we know as the near-death experience.

FINDING THE SOURCE

After the Seattle study, in which we determined that a person must be on the brink of death to have a near-death experience, we asked ourselves another question: What is the relationship of NDEs to hallucinations and other psychic phenomena?

We researched the medical literature and found that NDEs are unique. No other hallucinations, visions, or psychic phenomena are identical to NDEs. I have to say that I was surprised. I assumed that I would find many drugs that mimicked the experience. I was mystified to find that marijuana, psychedelics, alcohol, narcotics, anesthetic agents, Valium, lack of oxygen to the body, or severe psychological stress did not cause NDEs.

A form of gas therapy called the Medune mix did cause experiences similar to NDEs, but I believe that was because patients actually were near death from being forced to breathe a high concentration of carbon dioxide. This was done in the name of psychotherapy in the 1940s, as a possible cure for depression and other mental disorders. Treatment was halted when the expected results didn't occur.

Our research stumped me. I was not alone in my inability to find drug or psychological causes for NDEs. A number of researchers, including Raymond Moody, psychologist Kenneth Ring, and even astronomer Carl Sagan, could find no common pathway to explain the near-death experience—except near death, that is. Moody, the first medical doctor to study the near-death experience, concluded in a 1988 *Psychology Today* article that "for years I have been trying to come up with a physiological explanation for NDEs, and for years I have come up empty-handed."

My first hint of a solution to this problem came when I was casually discussing NDEs with Art Ward, former chairman of neurosurgery at the University of Washington. Ward is a great thinker, a surgical artist, and a crusty old man whose shoot-from-the-hip style causes many junior residents to cower in fear. He is not given to metaphysical thinking; "hard science" and just the facts are his domain. Yet when I described NDEs to him, he was already very familiar with them.

He had heard them recounted from many of his own patients.

Ward remembered one patient who experienced every trait of the near-death experience while Wilder Penfield poked an area of his brain with an electric probe. As part of the patient's brain was stimulated, he had the sensation of leaving his body. When another area close by was stimulated, he had the sensation of zooming up a tunnel, and so forth.

Ward thought that the area Penfield was probing was the right temporal lobe. He felt that some very interesting experiments could have been conducted had they thought of them at the time. For instance, they might have devised ways to see if these people were really leaving their bodies. Unfortunately, said Ward, nobody thought of it at the time.

This was an intriguing lead. Our team of researchers began to examine Penfield's work. Buried in a forty-year-old textbook, we found clear reference to areas of the brain that, when electrically stimulated, produced out-of-body experiences. At times patients on his operating table would say, "I am leaving my body now," when he touched this area with an electric probe. Several reported saying, "I'm half in and half out."

The area he was "mapping" was the Sylvian fissure, an area in the right temporal lobe located just above the right ear. When he electrically stimulated the surrounding areas of the fissure, patients frequently had the experience of "seeing God," hearing beautiful music, seeing dead friends and relatives, and even having a panoramic life review.

This was an exciting find. Up until this point, the existence of archetypes was only a theory from psychotherapist C. G. Jung, who described them as being psychological phenomena present in the genetic makeup of all people, regardless of race, creed, or color.

We were stumped. We had confirmed the specific area of the brain *where* NDEs occur, but we didn't know what was actually happening when they occurred.

Someone proposed that this experience was a defense mechanism, a way for the body to fool itself into believing that it was surviving death. That theory made sense to a point, but it didn't explain the reason that these experiences were so consistent from one NDEer to the next. After all, why would a person on the brink of death almost always have an experience that was so similar to what another person on the brink of death experienced? Why were they leaving their bodies, zooming up tunnels, seeing Beings of Light, and all those other things? Why weren't they having experiences so individual that they couldn't be categorized? That the distress of near death causes a neurological response almost explains it. But there is some research that couldn't be ignored.

The research on out-of-body experiences, which about twenty-five percent of NDEers have, represented very compelling evidence that *something* was leaving the body.

We discussed the research of Michael Sabom, an Atlanta cardiologist who has done some fascinating work on out-of-body experiences and people who almost died of cardiac arrest. In these experiences, a person in a near-death crisis claims to leave his body and watch his own resuscitation as the doctor performs it in the emergency room or during surgery. Sabom had thirty-two such patients in his study.

Sabom asked twenty-five medically savvy patients to make educated guesses about what happens when a doctor tries to get the heart started again. He wanted to compare the knowledge of "medically smart" patients with the out-of-body experiences of medically unsophisticated patients.

He found that twenty-three of the twenty-five in the control group made major mistakes in describing the resuscitation procedure. On the other hand, none of the near-death patients made mistakes in describing what went on in their own resuscitations. This presented very strong evidence that these people were actually outside their bodies and looking down as they said they were.

Sabom's research represented excellent empirical evidence of a life out-of-body, or at least an extremely sensitive sixth sense. So did many of the stories we had heard from patients and other doctors.

Dr. William Serdahely at Montana State University told us the remarkable story of an eight-year-old boy named Jimmy.

Jimmy was fishing from a bridge when he slipped from his perch on the railing and hit his head on a rock in the water below. The doctor's report says that Jimmy had stopped breathing and was without a pulse when a police officer pulled him from the deep water in which he had floated facedown for at least five minutes. The policeman performed CPR for thirty minutes until the hospital helicopter arrived, but he reported that the boy was dead on the scene when they started the rush to the hospital.

The boy lived. Two days later, he was out of his coma.

"I know what happened when I fell off that bridge," he told his physician, who related this story to us. He proceeded to describe his entire rescue in vivid detail, including the name of the police officer who tried to resuscitate him, the length of time it took for the helicopter to arrive on the scene, and many of the life-saving procedures used on him in the helicopter and at the hospital.

He knew all of this, he said, because he had been observing from outside his body the entire time.

It was not my intent to assess whether or not these children actually left their physical bodies during their near-death experiences. In every case in which children could provide details of what was going on outside their body at a time that they were unconscious, it was astonishing to me how accurate these details were. If two female physicians attended the resuscitation, the child would accurately report that fact. If they were nasally intubated, they were able to report that. If they were taken to other rooms for X rays or procedures, again, they were always accurate in their descriptions. This does not mean that they were actually outside their physical bodies, however, as comatose patients simply may have better abilities to perceive what is going on around them than we have previously understood.

Yet there is one case in which a teenager told me a fantastic story that was so unusual it had to have been an out-of-body experience. Rhonda was a fifteen year old who went into severe allergic shock as the result of an X-ray procedure. She was having an intravenous pyelogram to assess her kidney function. She suffered a cardiac arrest as a result of an allergic reaction to the radiopaque material used in the procedure.

When interviewed a year later, she told me that suddenly the room was dark. She could see herself illuminated by a soft light. She felt that she was floating above her body, perhaps on the ceiling. She saw her father pick her up and throw her over his shoulder and run to the emergency room. She said the radiologist was running after him. She was then resuscitated in the emergency room.

I interviewed the hospital personnel who were involved with the case, and all agreed that her description was accurate. Certainly a reasonable explanation for the accuracy with which she reported the unique events of her resuscitation is that she was actually out of her body during it.

Most NDEs involve leaving the physical body and traveling to the light. When this teenager told me of being carried by her father to the emergency room, I thought that this case would certainly be the exception to the accurate reports of other children. Yet when I investigated it, I found every detail she described to be true.

In 1986, when it came time to publish our findings about the anatomical location of near-death experiences, we entirely ignored the spiritual implications. We all agreed that bridging the gap between psychology and neurology was a big step in itself. As the head of neurology said, "Let's leave out any of that metaphysical stuff we were talking about." It was felt to be too controversial, too "far out."

THE SOUL HYPOTHESIS

Our paper was published in 1986 in the *American Journal of Diseases of Children* without the words "soul" or "spirit" appearing anywhere in it. Afterward, some of us continued to discuss this area of the brain in a different light. We began to ponder several questions: Does this information demystify the near-death experience? Does the fact that we know where the experience originates make it more a reflex than a spiritual experience?

We ultimately answered "no" to this question. Like Wilder Penfield and others who had done brain research, we now knew where in the brain a certain action took place; we didn't know why.

There are many other examples of genetic imprinting within the human brain, and none of those functions is any less valid for being inborn. For instance, we are all born with the capacity to learn language. This built-in language analyzer enables us to learn the language of our society. This ability to analyze language is genetically part of our brains, although it is strongly influenced by environment. Which is why the French speak French and Americans speak English with an American accent.

Birds are another example of animals that have genetically printed information in their brains. They are born with a detailed map of the night sky that is somehow passed to them through genetic tissue. Birds do not need to learn what the sky looks like; they come equipped with an inner map of the heavens. Using planetariums that can project a changing night sky, scientists have demonstrated that birds raised in labs and never exposed to the night sky are born with a "memory" of the stars that enables them to navigate.

Rather than diminish the NDE, we should consider the metaphysical ramifications of the phenomenon. As Penfield said: "I have no doubt the day will dawn when the mystery of the mind will no longer be a mystery. But I believe that one should not pretend to draw a final scientific conclusion, in man's study of man, until the nature of the energy responsible for mind-action is discovered."

CONFIRMING THE THEORY

When my research team published its report on the anatomy of the near-death experience, we were contacted by a group of neurologists in Chile who had been studying the same thing. They had arrived at the same anatomical conclusions that we did, that near-death experiences were generated by neuron activity within the Sylvian fissure. By examining the effects of a wide variety of psychoactive drugs, lack of oxygen, epileptic seizures, and altered states on the brain, the Chilean researchers pinpointed the same area in the brain as being the site of NDEs.

But exactly what did that discovery mean? They were as stumped as we were. They called for research that would study NDEs in the light of visionary experiences, for example, Paul's ecstatic visions and claims of astral travel. But for now, they said, "We are on the right path in separating physical elements from metaphysical ones."

I was excited to learn that two independent research teams had arrived at the same conclusion. Frankly, there were times when I worried that our anatomical theory was completely incorrect. Learning that other scientists had reached the same conclusion independently told us that we had at least discovered the circuit boards of mysticism. In our hearts, some of us believed strongly that we had discovered the seat of the soul.

THE HEAVENLY MIND

As so frequently happens, children can sum up difficult concepts with a few innocently spoken words. Such was the case with one child who spoke to researcher Elisabeth Kübler-Ross about death and the nature of the soul.

During a visit to Seattle, Kübler-Ross described a seven-year-old boy who asked his mother to turn off the oxygen so that he could finally die after a three-year battle against leukemia. "Turn off the oxygen; I don't need it anymore," he said. "It is my time."

He had experienced a predeath vision of what heaven was like. The vision revealed that his grandfather would be waiting for him. Despite his illness, he was excited about going to heaven.

When he was asked what heaven looked like in his vision, he tried his best to explain it: "It's sort of like if you went through another passageway . . . you walked right through a wall to another galaxy or something. It's sort of like walking into your brain. And it's sort of like living on a cloud, and your spirit is there, but not your body. You've left your body. It is really like walking into your mind."

This boy's experience represents the soul as being the place where the material and the spiritual worlds meet, a perfect description really for a soul that is rooted in the brain. For him, there was no contradiction between believing that heaven is in his mind and that he can leave his body and meet his grandfather in heaven.

There was no contradiction for Dr. Penfield, either. In one of his lectures on the brain, he tackled the question of the soul with a directness frequently used by senior statesmen to attack thorny issues. He readily admitted that the energy source that powers the mind is a total mystery. It fills us with the fire of life, and in the end, the wind of death blows it out like a candle, said Penfield. Then what happens?

"It is clear that, in order to survive after death, the mind *must* establish a connection with a source of energy other than that of the brain," said Penfield. "If during life (as some people claim) direct communication is sometimes established with the minds of other men or with the mind of God, then it is clear that energy from without can reach a man's mind. In that case, it is not unreasonable for him to hope that after death the mind may waken to another source of energy."

I love this quote, both for what it says and for what it implies. It says that the mind is one thing, the brain another, and that the brain cannot do what the mind does. It implies that people may communicate through the mind's energy with other people and/or God. And that when the body dies, the mind may be forced to rely upon another source of energy for its existence.

Is the near-death experience the beginning of the soul's journey to another source of energy? Maybe. If Penfield had questions about the nature of the soul, then I feel comfortable having them too. After all, he spent years mapping the brain and studying its functions, and yet he was unable to locate the source of the awesome energy that powers all living things. It left him somewhat frustrated, but accepting of the mystery of life: "It is obvious that science can make no statement at present in regard to the question of man's existence after death, although every thoughtful man must ask that question," said Penfield. "Whether the mind is truly a separate element or whether, in some way not yet apparent, it is an expression of neuronal action, the decision must await for further scientific evidence."

"I'M ALIVE!": A CASE STUDY

I have another story from one of my own patients. When I am wondering about the mysterious nature of the soul and the unknown energy that sparks our lives, I think about this case. It happened to a boy I'll call Ben. This "boy" is now a forty-seven-year-old policeman, but when he was fourteen, he developed a serious case of rheumatic fever and was hospitalized for weeks at Boston Children's Hospital.

His situation continued to worsen, until one day he began experiencing severe chest pains. They became worse and worse until he could ignore them no longer. He remembers speaking to the nurse and saying that something bad was happening. He saw her run from the room to get a doctor, and then he noticed something strange: He was able to follow her. He floated behind her as she explained the situation to a doctor and then followed them as they ran back into his room to look at his body. He realized that he was looking at his own body, hovering above the whole scene like a dispassionate observer.

He looked down and saw that he was linked to his body by a silver cord that was attached to his foot. That was the only connection that he seemed to have.

A few seconds earlier he had been in severe pain. Now he was floating painlessly above his body while doctors and nurses began their lifesaving cardiac resuscitation.

While he watched what was going on below him, he suddenly felt as though there had been a great increase in his intelligence. He became aware of two Beings of Light, one on either side, who stayed with him as he peacefully watched the frantic scene below. He says that the presence of these beings gave him a sense of peace, love, and understanding. It wasn't as though he "knew everything," Ben now says. "It was more like I suddenly realized that life is a lot more simple than most of us think."

The doctors were losing Ben, or at least his body. They had tried everything they knew and were now pushing a long needle into his chest to inject his heart with epinephrine. As he watched this desperate procedure, the Beings of Light on either side of him asked if he wanted to stay on earth or go with them. "I want to stay," he said, watching as the doctors waited for the epinephrine to kick in.

The beings left, and Ben watched as the doctors gave up and pulled a sheet over his face. He could hear people talking in the hallway, consoling the doctors and nurses who had just lost their young patient. A student nurse remained at his bedside, softly crying. She had worked with him throughout his long hospitalization, and they had gotten to know each other quite well.

Suddenly, the Beings of Light reappeared and told

him he could return to his body. Ben could hardly believe it. He thought he was dead, and from the looks of things, he was. Now the two spirits told him that he could return to his body, a body that had been left for dead by his physicians.

With what felt like a hiccup, Ben was back in his body. He threw the sheet from himself, pulled the needle from his chest, and shouted, "I'm alive!"

Recalling the story of Ben makes me realize how shallow is our understanding of the spiritual. We search and search for the source of spiritual experiences, mapping the brain to find where these phenomena occur. For the most part, we forget that it isn't so important how they happen as it is that they happen.

The great psychologist William James said that such mystical experiences as NDEs are so personal that they are beyond words. As he put it: "They are pure and simple, an experience of Light."

The source of this light may forever remain a mystery.

6

The Pure Light

Grown men may learn from little children, for the
hearts of little children are pure, and, therefore, the
Great Spirit may show to them many things which
older people miss.

Black Elk, Native American Spiritual Leader

There is one aspect of the near-death experience that
neuroscience hasn't been able to account for—the
Light. Nearly every near-death experience of children
(and about one fourth of those of adults) has in it an
element of light. They all report that the Light appears
at the final stages of the NDE, after they have had an
out-of-body experience or have traveled up the tunnel.

Those who experience the Light say that it is more
than just light. There is substance to it that "wraps"
them in a warmth and caring that they have never before felt. For some the voice of God comes from the
Light. Seeing the Light results in an incredible change

in attitude that effects many of them for the rest of their lives.

Where the rest of the experience is extraordinary, the Light makes it mystical. It is the "truth" of the near-death experience.

Describing the Light is difficult. Most of the patients I have spoken to describe it essentially as a pure light of unconditional love. Others call it "all-knowing," "all-forgiving," and "all-loving." One patient, twenty years after seeing the Light at age five, told me, "I will never forget that Light. It is with me all the time." Another patient who had an NDE as a child said to me: "Others have seen God, but I only saw a Light, a Light that I will never forget."

There is one particular anecdote that vividly illustrates the nature of this light and the power it has to alter people's lives. This story comes from a woman named Terry. As a child she accidentally ate several painkillers and nearly died. While lying in a coma, she left her body and traveled down a tunnel. She said it was as though water were in the tunnel, and she was making her way through this mystical river in a small boat.

The water was dark, but she was unafraid. Suddenly, she turned onto another branch of the river and passed under a glowing arch that led to a light "so beautiful that it couldn't be called just a light. It represented love and peace and happiness and complete and utter joy."

The Light was misty like a "glowing cloud." From inside it, she heard a voice that she perceived to be that of God. "I felt completely at peace and at one with it," she now says.

Although the Light had the feeling of unconditional love, "a feeling I was perfectly at home with," she knew that she could go no farther into it and still return to her earthly body.

That was when she decided to return.

Terry's voice broke with emotion as she shared the most baffling part of the experience. "When I came out of the coma in the hospital, I opened my eyes and saw pieces of the Light everywhere. I could see how everything in the world fits together."

THE UNEXPLAINED

The Light is the one element of the near-death experience that brain researchers can't even come close to explaining. The testimony of children is clear on this point: The Light is the key element of the NDE.

How can we scientifically explain this light after death? I do not know of any biochemical or psychological explanation for why we would experience a bright light as the final stage of bodily death.

The rigidly reductionistic among us could explain NDEs in the following manner: A person is faced with a lifethreatening event. He or she leaves the physical body and watches what is happening in a detached and depersonalized manner. This has many useful functions in that a person does not feel pain or panic and can even deny that his/her life is being threatened with death. As we know from the works of Wilder Penfield discussed in the previous chapter, this can sometimes be explained as the right temporal lobe being stimulated by a lack of oxygen.

Then there is a life review, seeing lights and people, hearing noises, having feelings of great joy and peace and seeing heavenly places. Surely, the skeptics say, these are simple psychological events that can be explained by examining the brain's organic processes.

As the brain begins its final dying process, there is a collapse of the visual fields and tunnel vision results. The eyes are no longer seeing, and the brain can no longer interpret what it sees. The tunnel becomes dark and the organism dies. This is possibly explained by some recent research as being an interruption of blood flow in the posterior cerebral artery, which feeds blood to the area of our brain responsible for sight.

And then—there's light! Where does this light come from? The brain has nearly stopped functioning. The psychological processes I've just described took place in a few minutes (although they seemed longer to the beholder), and now all mental functions have ceased. One would assume that the bodily functions would simply cease, that there would be eternal darkness.

Then why the Light?

I feel that I have done as much as anyone to outline the known neurological processes that can explain near-death experiences. Although many of the NDE elements can be explained by our knowledge of the way the brain works, the one that remains a true mystery is the experience of light.

Whereas most of the traits of the NDE can be precisely located in the anatomy of the brain, there is no explanation for what happens when the seat of consciousness travels through the tunnel and enters the Light. Like the birth of a child, it is the end product of an anatomical process that involves a voyage down a tunnel toward a world of color and brightness.

REBIRTH AT DEATH

Perhaps this light somehow represents a birth into a spiritual realm. After all, many of the anecdotes from children seem to indicate such a possibility.

A study done by Nancy Evans Bush contains stories that link the Light with rebirth. Here are some of the accounts from the mouths of the children from the International Association for Near-Death Studies (IANDS) in Connecticut. IANDS was founded in 1977 by Dr. Raymond Moody, Dr. Bruce Greyson, Dr. Michael Sabom, and Dr. Kenneth Ring. The purpose of the association is to bring an interdisciplinary approach to the near-death research. It now has hundreds of chapters worldwide.

Bush based her report on accounts in the archives of IANDS that were reviewed for obvious psychosis or delusions by Dr. Greyson, who is chief of psychiatry at the University of Connecticut.

In one of these accounts, a four-year-old girl, using a flashlight to go down the cellar stairs, stepped off the edge of the wrong side of the landing and fell to the cement floor far below. At a later age, she described what happened to her:

"The next thing I was aware of was being up near the ceiling over the foot of the stairs. The light was dim and at first I saw nothing unusual. Then I saw myself lying, facedown, on the cement, over to the side of the stairway. I was a little surprised, but not at all upset at seeing myself that way. I watched and saw that I didn't move at all. After a while, I said to myself, 'I guess I'm dead.' But I felt good! Better than I ever had. I realized I probably wouldn't be going back to my mother, but I wasn't afraid at all. . . .

"I noticed the dim light growing slowly brighter. The source of light was not in the basement, but far behind and slightly above me. I looked over my shoulder into the most beautiful light imaginable. It seemed to be at the end of a long tunnel which was gradually getting brighter and brighter as more and more of the Light entered it. It was yellow-white and brilliant, but not painful to look at even directly. As I turned to face the Light with my full 'body,' I felt happier than I ever had before or have since.

"Then the Light was gone. I felt groggy and sick, with a terrible headache. I only wanted my mother, and to stop my head from hurting."

"THE ENERGY OF THE UNIVERSE"

Another story collected by IANDS comes from a fourteen-year-old boy who was rescued from a car that was swept from a bridge by raging floodwaters. This is how he wrote about the incident several years later.

"I knew I was either dead or going to die. But then something happened. It was so immense, so powerful, that I gave up on my life to see what it was. I wanted to venture into this experience which started as a drifting into what I could only describe as a long, rectangular tunnel of light. But it wasn't just light, it was a protective passage of energy with an intense brightness at the end which I wanted to look into, to touch.

". . . As I reached the source of the Light, I could see in. I cannot begin to describe in human terms the feelings I had over what I saw. It was a giant infinite world of calm, and love, and energy, and beauty. It was as though human life was unimportant compared to this. And yet it urged the importance of life at the same time it solicited death as a means to a different and better life. It was all being, all beauty, all meaning for all existence. It was all the energy of the Universe forever in one place.

"As I reached my right hand into it, feelings of exhilarating anticipation overwhelmed me. I did not need my body anymore. I wanted to leave it behind, if I hadn't already, and go to my God in this new world."

"IT WAS WONDERFUL"

In this story, a nine-year-old girl had an NDE four hours after surgery for a ruptured appendix. Her parents were told that she would probably not live through the night so they were at her bedside watching as she saw the Light. She recalls the event with wonder:

"Then the blackness was gone and in its place was a beautiful soft pink light. All the weight was gone, and I floated back up into the room as light as a feather. I seemed to be filled with this same light, which was the most profound spirit of love that you can imagine. Nothing has ever come near it since. I opened my eyes, and the whole room was just bathed in that beautiful light. In fact, the Light completely surrounded everything in the room, there were no shadows. I felt so happy . . . I heard my father say, 'What's she looking at?' The Light lasted for a little while and it was wonderful.''

"THE LIGHT WOULD NOT HURT ME"

A woman named Carmen contacted me through a patient to tell of her experience at the age of five with the Light. She had been born with a congenital heart defect that had to be corrected with a complicated surgical procedure. While doctors tried to take her off the heart-lung machine, Carmen found herself above the operating table watching her own body being worked on. As she tells it:

"I suddenly realized that I could see myself on the operating table below! I knew there were problems because everyone seemed concerned that they couldn't get my heart to beat. It seemed strange to be able to see my own body down there, but it wasn't frightening.

"As I watched, I found myself floating up toward a bright light. It was very bright, but I wasn't afraid because I knew the Light would not hurt me. I was surrounded by it for a while, and then I sort of blended into my body. It was a wonderful feeling."

"I WANTED TO REACH THE LIGHT"

Pam is a thirty-nine-year-old graphic artist who had a cardiac arrest at the age of five after touching a live electrical wire. As she tells it:

> "I found myself falling down a tunnel with colored ridges that led down to a bright light. I fell slowly at first and then began to fall faster and faster. The faster I went, the better I felt. I wanted to reach the Light but I couldn't.
>
> "Even though I never reached the Light, I think it has changed the way I feel about life and death. It has certainly made me feel more spiritual and loving."

MORE THAN BRIGHTNESS

To understand the Light further, it is necessary to comprehend the power it can have to illuminate our lives. The experience of near-death researcher Michele Sorensen illustrates this point.

As a teenager she had injured her leg skiing, and her ligaments were surgically repaired. She developed a serious infection of the blood and bone afterward and nearly died. She was lying on the living room couch with three friends studying textbooks nearby when she suddenly felt as if she had left her body. The pain and fevered chills she had been experiencing were gone.

> "Suddenly I was above my body, looking down from a corner of the room. I felt a wonderful warmth

with no chills. A man was standing behind me. The warmth seemed to come from that person and spread around me. I did not turn around. I stared in relief at my form on the bed. I was at peace. I knew I was dead.

"Then I thought. 'I should have done this sooner!' Over the years, I have had a hard time explaining how this man talked to me. Yet he did, and the communication was so warm and loving and so peaceful, that I knew the radiant white light was his love. He knew what I had been through, and his compassion put me at rest.

" 'You are dead, you know,' he said.

" 'Yes, I know. It's great!'

" 'Do you truly want to be dead?'

" 'Oh yes. Why not, this is all so wonderful.' I thought of the Light and the love.

"Looking down at myself on the bed below, I saw my friend put her hand to my body's forehead and then neck to find a pulse. She was screaming. Other people were shouting. 'She's dead, she's dead.'

"I saw my mother's face and my brother's face. He was overseas and they were calling him. I saw a whole network of phone lines, with people's faces on the phones. I felt sad that they were upset, but felt that they would get over it. Even my mother and father would want me to have release from the pain I was having.

" 'But look what you are missing,' the voice said.

"I saw a tall blond man walking with two children. The little girl jumped up and down and her curls shook. The other was a boy. I recognized this as being my future family. I felt a longing for my husband and children even before I had met them!

"The bliss I felt as a dead person suddenly felt

temporary. I began to waiver about the joys of being dead before I had even experienced the fullness of life. 'Yes I want to go back,' I said. And I went back."

The Light changed Michele's life, or as she puns, it "enlightened" her. As with so many others who have had this spiritual experience, the world made more sense after seeing the Light. Things fit together coherently. Most of all, life seemed to have real purpose. "I realized that death was not to be feared," said Michele. "The only real fear is in not accomplishing our work in this life." By the way, Michele is married to a former basketball player who is blond. They have two children, a boy and girl.

THE DIVINE LIGHT

Notice how these experiences of light have a religious quality to them? It has long been my belief that many of the world's great religious leaders have been driven by profound near-death and other visionary experiences that involve the mystical light. There are many such examples—both great and small—of people being turned toward a life of devotion by the Light. Usually these occur during childhood.

One of my own patients had such an experience at the age of fifteen. He "died" of a severe infection. While doctors rushed to begin heart massage, he saw a light at the end of his bed. It grew larger and larger until it totally engulfed him. Then from the brightness came a "wonderfully kind" face that was thousands of years old yet without wrinkles. He was frightened by what he saw, a fear that was eliminated when the man touched his forehead.

After that he knew he wanted to become a minister. Now, thirty years later, he is a mainstream Protestant minister who "brings that vision of the Light" to others.

Native American spiritual leader Black Elk had a near-fatal illness at age nine that put him in touch with the Light.

The illness he described resembles rheumatic fever. He says that he had a high fever and swollen joints. He had a long and detailed experience rich with religious imagery and visions of dead relatives. The very heart of his experience occurred when he was on the highest mountain of them all, and beneath him was the entire world. A bright light surrounded the earth, "wide as daylight."

In *Autobiography of a Yogi*, the Indian guru Paramahansa Yogananda describes his near-death experience at age eight, which then enhanced his lifelong devotion to religion.

In that autobiography he states: "There [was] a blinding light, enveloping my body and the entire room. My nausea and other uncontrollable symptoms disappeared; I was well." This light then stayed with him the rest of his life, and he was able to illuminate others with it.

The religious implications of the Light were described more than two hundred years ago by Jonathan

Edwards, the Calvinist theologian who put forth the belief that "there is such a thing as a spiritual and divine light, immediately imparted to the soul by God, of a different nature from any obtained by natural means." He describes this light as having "no impression upon the mind, as it is not seen with the bodily eyes. It can be described as thus: a spiritual and saving conviction of the truth and reality of divine glory. It is sweet and pleasant to the soul."

The Light, Edwards said, enables us to "see the mutual relations between things and occasions us to take more notice of them."

How did Edwards know about the Light more than two centuries ago? In researching his life, I found that he had nearly died of pleurisy as a child, an illness that may well have led to a near-death experience.

All of these examples are not to say that one has to have a near-death experience to see the Light. Oxford scholar Edward Robinson reports on a spiritual experience he had as a four-year-old: "My mother and I were walking on a stretch of land known locally as the moors. As the sun declined and the slight chill of evening came on, a pearly mist formed over the ground. Suddenly I seemed to see the mist as a shimmering gossamer tissue and flowers appearing here and there, seemed to shine with a brilliant fire. Somehow I understood that this was the living tissue of life itself, in which what we call consciousness was embedded: appearing here and there was a shining focus of energy in that more diffused whole. In that moment I knew that I had my own special place, as had all other things.

"The vision has never left me, and with it the same intense feeling of love of the world and the certainty of ultimate good."

Obviously this is not a near-death experience. The child is not physically or emotionally threatened with death. There is no separation from the physical body, no out-of-body experience, and no tunnel. This is clearly a spiritual experience, not an NDE.

Nonetheless, I think the Light seen during NDEs and the mystical light seen by those having a spiritual experience are the same light. Both fuel religious awe and both have the power to transform. As psychologist William James said in his *Varieties of Religious Experience*, the hallmark of religious experience involves "a sense of being bathed in a warm glow of light. Earth, heaven and sea resounding as in one vast world-encircling harmony." I have heard young children struggling to explain the same thing to me about the Light at the end of the tunnel.

There are several ways to tap this spiritual energy. My guess is that the psychic powers to do so exist in all of us and that given the time and desire we could see the Light without having to die for it.

Still, most of these experiences of light happen to the most innocent among us, the children. And in their simple way, these experiences are expressed with eloquence. No priest or rabbi could be so eloquent.

BUT WHERE IS THE LIGHT?

The question of great interest is: Where is the Light located? Is it outside the body, representing a place that we go? Or is it just a flash of primal energy within our brains, a sort of supernova of the ego, perhaps?

This has not been my primary question in researching near-death experiences. My research has been aimed at helping the patient work closer with the medical team and at understanding the deep workings of our psyches that affect the dying process. Through my work I would like to prevent what Dr. Mary Robinson at Children's Hospital in Washington, D.C., called "[the turning] away from the dying patient and family" that is done by physicians and their support staff. It has been my hope that these near-death experiences will teach us all how to listen to each other, will break down the walls of isolation and grief that shield us from death.

However, in the course of conducting this more grounded research, I have come to believe that the Light is located outside our bodies.

When I began my research, I never would have dreamed that I would write these words. But the testimony of children and many of their unexplainable encounters have convinced me.

THE STORY OF JUNE

A young girl we'll call June first made me think the Light was not just located in the mind. She was an eight-year-old patient of mine who nearly drowned in Seattle's Puget Sound when she fell out of her father's fishing boat.

On an overcast day, she flipped over the gunwales and sank twenty feet to the sandy bottom. Her father turned the boat around, and a close family friend jumped into the murky water and began searching for her. Three times he dove to the bottom of the sound, possessed by the strength and heroism that an emergency can evoke. He could see nothing because of the turbulent waters and the overcast day.

On the fourth dive, he suddenly saw her body. He described it as "illuminated from within" by a soft bright light. This man told me later that he had "a sense of awe and reverence." He pulled her lifeless body from the depths, and they raced her to a hospital. Despite being underwater for at least twenty minutes, she lived.

A few days later, both men returned to the site with scuba gear. The man who saved June had told everyone about the Light. Now he wanted to see just how much natural light actually reached the bottom of the sound on a sunny day.

Both men dove down and both said that they could see only a few feet in front of their eyes.

I believe that she was having an NDE and that both she and her rescuer were seeing the Light at the same time.

THE SAVING LIGHT

There have been other instances in which the Light has intervened to save children.

In 1986, David Young and his family carried an arsenal of weapons and a bomb into an elementary school in Cokeville, Wyoming. After holding 156 children hostage and threatening to kill them all, Young detonated the bomb, destroying the entire school. None of the children was harmed.

How did this miracle of survival happen?

Many of the children described seeing people of light who directed them to safety before the explosion occurred. Others talked about hearing the voice of an adult who told them where to go to avoid the bomb's blast.

One girl described her experience in detail: "They [the people of light] were standing there above us. There was a mother and a father and a lady holding a tiny baby and a little girl with long hair. There was a family of people. The woman told us that a bomb was going off soon and to listen to our brother. She said to be sure we did what he told us. They were dressed in white, *bright like light bulbs, but brighter around the face*. The woman made me feel good. I knew she loved me."

The girl's brother stated: "I didn't see anything. I just heard a voice tell me to find my little sisters and take them over by the window, and keep them there. They were playing with their friends, and they did not

want to move. I took them to the window and helped
them through.''

Another six-year-old child also testified that ''a
lady told me that a bomb was going to go off
soon. She said to go over by the window and hurry
out.''

Sheila contacted me after hearing me lecture at a
local hospital. Twenty years before, she said, at the
age of twelve, she'd had a near-death experience as a
result of a near drowning. She probably would have
drowned, she says, had a ''guardian light'' not rescued her from the deep water. She tells the story:

  ''In the 1950s I lived in the Cedar River area of
  Washington State. Several friends and I were jump-
  ing off the clay bank of the river into an area that
  was safe to swim in. We knew the dangerous areas
  of the river and normally avoided them.
  ''On this particular day, I became careless and
  rather than wait my turn and jump into the safe
  area, I decided to jump into a particularly dangerous
  spot, a twenty-foot hole that had a sucking whirlpool.
  ''I was pulled down and then I came up. I could
  see people panicking and trying to reach me from
  the shore with branches, but the pull of the water
  was too great, and nobody was coming close to
  reaching me. As I came up for the third time, I
  remembered the old saying that a drowning person
  comes up for air three times. I was getting very
  tired. I felt that I was being pulled down again. This
  time though I felt as though I was standing still on
  the bottom. A few feet from me appeared a rectangular light which was brilliant but very soft at the

same time. Nothing in the world mattered at that time. It was a moment of euphoric peace.

"I remember reaching out for the Light. But before I had a chance to touch it, I was transported to the shore. I know I wasn't swimming to the shore. The Light picked me up and took me there."

Ever since this experience, Sheila has felt a personal mission to study man's purpose on earth. She says: "I try to get on with my mundane life and not get too serious, but the sense of responsibility and higher purpose is always there." She doesn't understand how people can take their lives for granted. "Most people don't realize how precious life is," she says.

She feels that people who have had near-death experiences should come together and try to get others to find purpose in life. "The Light convinced me that there is more to life than most people experience."

This type of dramatic yet verifiable evidence of the Light intervening in our lives is extraordinarily rare. It is difficult for me to believe even when I read eyewitness accounts of those who were present or—in the cases of Cher and Sheila—actually interview the witnesses myself. It is frequently hard for the witnesses to believe. With Cher, for instance, her father and the rescuer could hardly believe that the Light had originated from within her in a supernatural fashion, even though the man who saved her swears he saw it. Indeed, we find it hard to believe in something we cannot understand. Yet still these experiences of Light happen.

THE OTHER GRANDMOTHER

This story comes to me from a professional acquaintance.

A family was caring for their dying grandmother. In addition to the ravages of old age (she was in her eighties), she had arthritis and heart disease.

The parents discouraged their daughter from spending too much time around the grandmother. They felt that the rapid deterioration of a family member was too horrible a sight for their nine-year-old child to witness.

One day, the child was drawn to the grandmother's room. She went in for a few minutes and then came out with a puzzled look on her face. "Mommy," she said. "There are two grandmothers. I saw two grannies in the room. First I talked to granny and then a lighted lady named Beth came and talked to me and granny. Then they left together."

The mother and daughter went into the room and discovered that the grandmother had died. This was a very convincing experience for the mother. The genuine manner with which the event was presented by the daughter was evidence enough for her. The mother felt that further proof was provided by the "lighted" granny named Beth. For Beth was the name of her great-grandmother, someone the little girl had not heard about.

Could this light, seen by the person having a near-death experience and occasionally seen by others, be a physical manifestation of our guardian angel or guiding light? Many children have described guardian angels who are blond or "all white" who escort them to heaven.

For example, this full-blown near-death experience happened to a child who had a reaction to antibiotics that put her into anaphylactic shock, a sometimes fatal reaction to drugs.

She had an out-of-body experience, went up a tunnel, saw a paradise of light, and was engulfed by a "Godlike light." During this spiritual journey, she also met a guardian angel named Sarah.

This near-death experience occurred twenty years ago. Yet remarkably, Sarah has never left this woman's side. During periods of stress, Sarah reappears to provide solace and advice.

The woman and Sarah have had in-depth discussions about several earthly problems, including marital strife, job difficulties, the travails of raising children. When she needs her, Sarah is always there. All this woman needs to do is sit alone in a quiet place and ask for her presence.

Until recently my patient thought that Sarah was invisible. Then a remarkable thing happened. She was having extraordinary problems with her teenage son, who was failing school, staying out late at night, and being generally rebellious in the worst of teenage traditions. Waiting up for him to return from a night on the town, my patient sat in her darkened family room and "called-up" Sarah.

For the next half hour, the woman and her guardian angel had a heart-to-heart talk about the difficulties of raising teenage boys. Little did my patient know that her son had come home and had witnessed half of their discussion, watching the angel and his mother talk as he peeked around a corner.

In the morning, he confronted her with what he had seen. "Mom," he said. "Who was that woman you were talking to last night? She seemed real nice."

What else could my patient do? She told her son about her constant companion, Sarah. She then sought me out because of my interest in NDEs. She said she needed a medical opinion as to her sanity. Did I think she was crazy? After talking to her for a while, I had to say that I didn't think she was crazy at all.

"What am I?" she then asked.

I thought for a moment. "Lucky, I guess."

BRIGHT NEW BEGINNING

According to science, death should mean the extinction of life and light. Biologically speaking, we should close our eyes at the end of life's process and that should be it, extinction of consciousness, absence of light.

We know—especially from the experiences of children—that such an extinction does not occur in a near-death situation. These children tell us that there is a darkness, an end to the light we experience every day. But then there is another light, one that represents love and has "a lot of good things for me in it," as one boy told me.

This light is the core near-death experience and cannot be explained by any scientific theories. I have documented the anatomical areas of the brain where the source of NDEs is located. But there is no scientific explanation for the Light. All we know is that, at the point of death, a brilliant, beautiful, loving, and peaceful light awaits us.

Many patients describe the Light as continuing on, even after the near-death experience is over. One patient said that whenever she fell asleep as a child she would reexperience the Light. Another described her near-death experience at age two: "I saw a bright light that I knew was God. I had the deepest possible experience from being in the Light. When I was a youngster, I could still see sparkles in a dark room from when I first saw that light."

Children even draw pictures of the Light. In fact, when I ask children to draw pictures of what happened during their near-death experience, they almost always include a representation of the Light.

It is fascinating to me that these children, sometimes as young as two and three years old, use the same descriptions of the Light as the previously mentioned spiritual leaders use in their descriptions of the Light of God.

If we assume that this experience of the Light is simply a spasm of rigor mortis in the optic nerve, then how can we account for all of the higher order processing of unconditional love, total truth, and feelings of deep peace and joy? If it is a final death spasm of the optic nerve, patients would simply say: "I saw a blinding bright light."

Using Freud's model of the mind, some psychologists have attempted to explain the Light as merely the internalized parents—the superego—coming to the rescue in the form of the Being of Light.

Although that is as good an explanation as I have ever heard for the Light, it still leaves much to be explained. If the Light is merely a product of superego, why is it sometimes visible outside the dying person's body?

There are more questions than answers when dealing with the Light. I would like to believe that the Light is where we go when we die. Like a birth into a bright new world, the Light of the NDE represents the beginning of a new beginning.

7

Transformation

He who would teach men to die, would teach them to live.

—*Montaigne*

It has been eight years now since I first met Katie. The little girl who was so close to death from drowning that the pupils of her eyes didn't respond to bright light is now a lovely teenager who seems normal in every way.

I have stayed in close contact with Katie and her family. Her parents think that she is as charming and bright as a teenage girl can be. But Katie's parents have six children, and they think *all* of them are model kids. Which isn't to say that Katie's experience hasn't had a profound effect upon her life. It did. Katie and her parents feel that her NDE made her a different person in many ways.

Katie feels that God sent her back to be a help to her mother. She has been just that. She is an extraordinarily mature fifteen-year-old who helps her mother run a large household. She has a part-time job, gets good grades, excels in ballet, and has never taken drugs. "Why would I need drugs?" she asks, wrinkling her nose in disbelief at the question.

These effects on Katie intrigued me. I began to wonder about adults who'd had NDEs during childhood. Did they embellish their experiences as they became adults until they were more fiction than fact? And what about the effects of those NDEs on their lives? Do they feel "chosen" or "special"? Do they think they have greater insights because of their spiritual experiences?

"BEFORE AND AFTER": CASE STUDY

I searched my files for cases of people who had had near-death experiences as children and again as adults to see if there were differences in the NDEs.

Since I have discussed this topic on several television and radio programs, many people have contacted me. At first I was puzzled by this. Why were they calling me when they had already told their stories dozens of times? Then I realized that they wanted a sympathetic ear from the medical community. For the most part, they had been ignored by their doctors when they told of their marvelous journeys—sometimes they were even ridiculed or diagnosed as temporarily insane. They came to me for acceptance from a physician.

Rather than treat these patients as though something

were wrong with them, I listen willingly, jotting notes while they tell me their intriguing stories. Later I consult with their physicians or check their medical records to make sure they didn't have histories of mental problems.

I found in my files two patients who each had two NDEs, one as a child and the other as an adult. The first case concerns a woman who, at the age of two, had an NDE while suffering from pneumonia and, at the age of sixty-nine, her second after a cardiac arrest. Here, in her own words, are both of the experiences:

"When I was two, I had measles and then came down with pneumonia as a result. That was in the days before antibiotics, and the doctor said that there was nothing he could do for me. I don't remember hearing him say that, especially since I was only two. But it's amazing what I do remember.

"My mother was making a poultice for my chest when I suddenly 'died.' The doctor was there and he began shaking me. It turned dark all around me, and then I saw a bright light that I knew was from God. I had the deepest possible experience from being in the Light. I felt love and comfort. I wasn't frightened. I only wondered, 'Oh my, how will I get back in my body?' Then suddenly I was back in, looking up at my mother and the doctor.

"When I got older, I could still see sparkles from that light whenever I was in a dark room. It kept me from being afraid."

Sixty-two years later this woman had another NDE. Here is her vivid description of that experience.

"I was over at the garage getting my car fixed when suddenly—*boom*—I was out of my body. It happened so fast. The mechanic just stared at me. I have never been able to get him to talk about what he saw in me that day. Whenever I bring it up he always says "no problem, no problem" and sort of backs away.

"This was the beginning of all my heart problems. But it really wasn't such a bad way to begin. I was part in and part out of my body. I then had the most marvelous time bouncing in and out of my body. And then, all of a sudden, I was in a velvety black place. But I wasn't frightened, since I was always there with, well, God. And I wasn't dreaming. I was in a black void and I knew I was dead but I wasn't frightened.

"Then suddenly there came a fog, and right in the center was my beautiful amber light. I was filled with complete knowledge and wonderment. I felt as though I was skating and that if I could just go out there and skate a pattern that it would be the most beautiful pattern of all.

"I could only imagine that God was with me and that he controlled everything I saw and thought. It was so glorious to be up there with him. There was an amber light and above it a huge angel—I think it was my guardian angel.

"To the right of the Light was a huge plank, a giant four-by-four, which stretched beside me. It was covered with a horrible green paint. I didn't want to touch it because it was my barrier. God told me that if you are meant to go back, they put up a barrier. Sometimes it's a cliff, sometimes it's a waterfall. Mine was a green plank like you see in a trick or treat place.

"Then he took me into the Light. Light was

pouring through me. My cheeks were bulging out. It was most delicious, a wonderful experience of that light passing through me.

"And then the plank came in front of me, and God was laughing behind me. He took my hand and put it on the plank. I looked down into a round opening in the black void in which people were walking around in white robes. Some people remained in the void, especially if they had committed suicide. He said, 'You can't go down there.'

"I then knew that I was going to return to my body. I knew I was so sick that I would never make it, but I was given no chance. I came back to the world."

The second case study of a patient who had an NDE as a child and again as an adult is a woman I'll call Paula. She wrote to me to report her childhood experience after a lecture I gave in Seattle.

"I had an NDE as a child that was extremely simple. When I was nine years old, I was put under anesthesia to have teeth removed. I had a cardiac arrest as a result of an allergic reaction to the anesthetic. I saw myself rolled into a very tight ball of light. I saw myself being hurled at a very great speed through a conical-shaped space. The ball was rotating at a very high speed and glowing with a warm, bright light. Sticking out from the ball were a hand and foot. That is all I can remember."

I spoke with her later to hear about her adult experience, which happened sixteen years later when she was twenty-five. She had just had a child and had been hospitalized for severe high blood pressure associated with pregnancy. At three A.M. on the second day of her stay, Paula awoke with the sense that the air in the hospital room was very heavy. She struggled to the door, opened it, and then fell backward. Hospital records show that she had a cardiac arrest due to a heart attack.

Paula says that there was no pain associated with the heart attack. She first went into a black void and then felt as though she had left her body and was able to watch everything from a position near the ceiling. She tells the rest:

"I was looking down at nurses who gathered around my body. There were three. One began taking my pulse and then yelled to the other two, 'Call a doctor, call her husband.' A doctor showed up almost immediately and after a brief examination said, 'She's dying.' I was able to go out into the hallway and see my aunt. She was a nurse in the same hospital and was standing outside my room talking to some patients from other rooms. 'What a shame,' she said. 'She was such a good little mother.' I was puzzled by the fact that they were talking about me in the past tense. I tried to talk to them, to tell them I was there, but I couldn't communicate with them.

"I was even able to go into the next room, where another patient was complaining about all the noise. The nurse there was saying, 'Well, Paula is seriously ill next door.' I then went back to my body in time to see my husband, who had just arrived. He was watching the doctor and saying, 'What am I going to tell the children?'

"I then thought that I might be dead. My next thought was not fear, but the feeling that this might be a neat experience. I wanted to tell them that I was there, that I could listen to them and watch them, but I couldn't talk to them or communicate in any way. It was frustrating.

"As I watched them work on my body, the room became very light. Then a canopy of color grew above me, like the canopy that is over the front door of a nightclub. It was made of blue and silver rain, and there was a very bright light in the middle of it. The air sparkled around this light, and I knew that the Light was where I wanted to go.

"From this light came other people. There was no 'God' or spiritual guide with them, only these ordinary people like myself who were people of light.

"I could go toward the Light yet come back to my body at the same time. It was literally like having one foot in eternity or being able to drift back and forth through the looking glass like the little girl in *Alice in Wonderland*.

"Finally, I came back to look down at my body, and I saw a doctor shaking my shoulder saying, 'Paula, Paula, come back.' That was when I came back into my body and awoke."

These experiences illustrate the flavor of childhood experiences as compared to those of adults. Research done by Nancy Evans Bush at the International Association for Near-Death Studies has shown that childhood NDEs are very similar to those of adults in that they contain the core experience of leaving the body, being in a void, and then being encompassed by the Light. The striking difference was the lack of a life review. In the seventeen childhood NDEs Bush examined, not one had a life review. Yet the other events were every bit as powerful as any found in the adult literature.

For instance, a ten-year-old boy who was sick for several weeks with an unidentified illness (the patient didn't know exactly what he had) experienced an NDE shortly after the doctors had "given up." Here is how he described it years later.

"I don't remember the entrance, but in a little while I was in a dark tunnel. There was absolutely no sound, and all was black. I couldn't see to make my way through the tunnel, but I was being wafted along as a speck of dust, pitch black, but as I went along with neither sight nor sound, I felt at ease. It seemed as though I was discovering a new cave.

"After a while the tunnel became square and seemed very long. I became annoyed and thought to myself that the journey was pointless and fruitless and I was wasting valuable time. Just when I was about to turn back in disgust (I was completely alone) I saw a tiny speck of light ahead. I went on, and as I did the speck grew larger, and I thought it was well I hadn't turned back because I was going to discover something at last.

"At about 150 yards from the end, I saw plainly that there was brilliant white light out there beyond the square end of the tunnel. It interested me and I went on. All was yet quiet, and I went blissfully on, enjoying the journey at last.

"When I was about twenty-five yards from the end, the Light became the most brilliant I have ever seen, yet it did not hurt my eyes. I began to wonder about that light because all I could see was light: no landscape, no people, nothing but a bright sea. And not a single ray entered the tunnel. The tunnel was black right to the end, and there was the sea of light.

"I went closer, cautious now because it seemed that the end of the tunnel was pretty high up on the side of a cliff, and since I couldn't see through the Light, I didn't know how far the drop might be if I left the tunnel. When I was near the end, I took a good look around at the sea of light. I was urged to jump into it and assured that I would not fall to the ground. No voice said this: it just came to me from a kind of presence. I thought it might be fun to try, but in an instant, I knew that if I left the end of the tunnel I'd never find it again and hence never get back home.

"I turned around and started back through the tunnel, and that is the last I remember."

In another case used by Bush, a nine-year-old girl had slipped off the high board at summer camp and had plunged into the ocean, where she stayed on the bottom for ten minutes before being rescued by a lifeguard.

"The next thing I remember is floating only an inch or two from the ocean's sandy bottom in the midst of a great light. The Light wasn't the bright glaring sort of light that makes you blink. Instead it was incandescent, almost ethereal. I could see every indentation and curvature in the sand and minute details in the seaweed. If there were fish or shells, I don't remember them. I felt absolutely nothing. Not the water, nor the sand, nothing. I was surrounded by silence, but I wasn't afraid. I wanted to stay there forever. I have never since experienced such a feeling of peace.''

As you can see, these experiences contain the same elements as adult NDEs. In Bush's analysis of the data, she found that children's experiences are the same as adults except they don't have a life review. In none of the childhood experiences that she examined was a life review present, where it is a feature of twenty-five percent of adult NDEs.

Why was there no life review present? Bush doesn't attempt to answer this question in her study. However, I believe that the reason children don't have a life review is simply that they don't yet have much of a life. After all, how much life does a seven-year-old child have to review?

A STUDY OF STORIES

I decided to research the stories of adults who had had NDEs as children. This type of research is known as anecdotal and is simply the analysis of stories gathered in a methodical fashion. That isn't to say that this type of research isn't valuable in a scientific sense. Many scientific advances have been made by anecdotal research. Virtually all of our infant-feeding practices, for instance, have been developed through anecdotal research. This type of research is often an important step that precedes larger controlled studies.

Another scientific advance inspired by anecdotal research has been the fluoridation of water to prevent tooth decay. This revolutionary advance in preventive dentistry was initiated by reports of children in Texas who mysteriously had few cavities. When a local dentist speculated that it was related to the concentration of minerals in the drinking water, he was widely ridiculed. Decades later, his anecdotal research is recognized as heralding one of the great medical advances of our time.

In addition, the use of aspirin to prevent heart attacks is the result of anecdotal research. This widely acclaimed preventive measure was first discovered by a general practitioner who noticed that patients being treated for arthritis with aspirin had fewer heart attacks than the general population. That anecdotal information has now been scientifically confirmed many times and has saved tens of thousands of lives.

Aware of the validity of anecdotal research, I devised a study to interview self-referred patients about their childhood NDEs. The people with whom I spoke were from such various professions as a scientist, an insurance claims adjuster, and a graphic artist. Some had only completed eleventh grade, some were high school graduates, and others had graduated from college. Although most had been raised as Christians, none was particularly religious. They all described themselves as being "typically middle class." All of them, of course, had to have suffered a near-fatal event that could be verified by hospital records. None could be mentally ill or drug users.

It was reassuring to see that our patients came from all walks of life. That way we could be certain that we were getting a good representation of what childhood NDEs are like, without the patients as a whole being biased by one particular life-style.

We were also careful not to bias the patients by the questions we asked. The interviews were completely open-ended and nondirected. Typical of the questions were these:

- What do you remember about your experience?
- Tell me about it.
- What happened next?

Such sparse questioning would prevent the patient from being "led by the nose" (as a colleague put it) toward some experience that might not have happened.

As a further control, I had the help of Kim Clark, a clinical instructor at the University of Washington and teacher of a course on death and dying. Although we used the same basic questionnaire, we worked separately. This enabled me to compare the types of anecdotes that Kim Clark collected with the type that I collected so that we could check our methods of questioning patients. If our results were significantly different, then we would know that one of us was doing our job wrong.

Despite differences in training, sex, personality, and even very different opinions as to the meanings of NDEs, our results were very similiar.

I would like to present some of the fascinating stories from these patients, with my conclusions.

THE THRONE OF GOD

Tom is a scientist of international reputation in his forties who nearly drowned at the age of five. He was pulled from a swimming pool and resuscitated by a relative. When the family finally got him to the hospital, doctors in the emergency room said he was dead. Shortly thereafter, he spontaneously revived.

> "When I went underwater, the next thing I remembered was passing down a long tunnel. The Light went from being very harsh to so bright that I could feel it. Then I saw God on a throne. People—maybe angels—were below looking up at the throne.
> "I sat on the lap of God, and he told me that I had to go back. 'It's not your time,' he said. I wanted to stay but I came back."

Tom credits this experience with "sorting out" his life. From that point on, he was driven to acquire knowledge. He decided to study science and engineering, subjects that could help him discover "the natural order of things."

His reputation shows that he has been successful in that endeavor.

THE HAND OF GOD

Kathleen is a bright forty-three-year-old who graduated from high school and has worked for the munic-
ipality where she has lived for twenty years. She has
dabbled in a number of faiths but believes only in a
vague conception of God.

When she was nine years old, she was walking on
a log in shallow water. Suddenly, the log turned, and
she slipped underneath it into the cold water. The log
pressed her into the soft mud of the riverbank and held
her head underwater for a long period of time. This is
how she describes the experience:

> "Suddenly, I felt very warm. Although I was
> facedown in cold water, I was suddenly under a
> cloudless, baby blue sky with a large fluffy circle
> glowing in it. From inside the circle came a hand.
> It was reaching for me, and the voice behind it was
> that of a woman. I couldn't understand what she was
> saying, but I knew she was anxious for me to come
> into the next world.
>
> "I withdrew my hand because I didn't want to
> go. I was lucky to have been brought back to life."

It is amazing how much change can come to a person's life even after such a fragmentary experience.
The reason Kathleen has dabbled in so many religions is that the God she sensed in the Light was not
the God perceived by the many religions with which
she has been involved. "The rules of religion are put
there by people," she said. "From my brief encoun-

ter, I got the idea that being one with God is something that can be done without rules.''

"NOT YOUR TIME"

Bill is a fifty-year-old who had his near-death experience at the age of nine while working on his family farm. He was siphoning gas out of a tractor when he accidentally inhaled it. Inhaled gasoline can cause rapid, or *fulminating*, pneumonia, which, in this case, cut off his oxygen. As his brother began screaming for help, Bill fell to the ground and quickly blacked out. He recalled:

> "All of a sudden I couldn't move. I found myself floating into a dark tunnel. I saw light and the closer I floated to it, the more I liked it. When I got to the portal opening to the Light and was just ready to step through, I felt a combination of relief, joy, and pleasure. I just wanted to be inside the Light.
>
> "Suddenly, a hand reached out and grabbed me. 'He's a feisty rascal, isn't he,' said a voice. 'Well, Bill, it's not your time this time. You have a job to do.'
>
> "Suddenly, I was above my body. I saw my brother below me. I saw my father rush to him and I heard him say, 'My God, my God.' I felt okay. I wasn't afraid. Then I saw my brother racing across the fields. I saw my dad shaking me, and I was spitting out gasoline and gagging and choking and then I came to.''

When I asked Bill what this experience meant to him over the years, he quickly pointed out that he has never been afraid to die. "I know that where we are going is a beautiful place," he said. "Because of that I have never carried that burden of fear with me that many people have about death."

Did he think he was being saved for something special? Bill shook his head. "I've been married thirty years, raised five children, and built my own company to the success it is today. To me that seems special."

MADNESS OR CLARITY?

Victor is a fifty-five-year-old engineer who is married and has two children. He is a veteran of World War II, during which he was diagnosed by Army psychologists as being schizophrenic and received a medical discharge. He has held a job and worked since that time. He has never been hospitalized for the condition, nor has he taken drugs for it. I include him here because I really doubt that diagnosis. I think he was labeled a schizophrenic because of his NDE. Here is Victor's story:

"When I was five, I had very bad pneumonia. It became so bad that my heart stopped. Suddenly, I floated out of my body! 'I didn't know you could do that,' I said. I saw my own body and people around me. Then I found myself traveling down a tunnel and headed for a light! Then I saw him, the Messiah!

"I can't really describe him or explain, but I just

knew it was the Messiah. He said, 'We will meet again,' and I came back to my body.''

As a direct result of this experience, Victor became very religious. He has a deep longing to "see God" again. The mistake he made was to tell Army psychiatrists about this deep longing after the war, when he was sent to them for battle fatigue. On the basis of that "confession" he was diagnosed as schizophrenic, someone who has had an acute break with reality.

Based upon his life-style over the last forty years, I am willing to say that he isn't mentally ill. He isn't medicated. He is happily married. He raised a family. He has held the same job for many years. He has never had another vision of God (nor anything else) since that brief yet powerful experience when he was five.

It is a pity that someone knowledgeable about NDEs wasn't able to counsel him. He was glad to talk to me because I didn't think he was mentally ill. He said that, although he never felt abnormal, the diagnosis left him feeling very peculiar about himself.

This man's story reminds me of a Tibetan tale of spiritual enlightenment that I have heard many times. A man ventured into the forest to live the life of a simple holy man. He craved enlightenment and sought the meaning of life by studying books and consulting with the wise men of Tibet. Still he felt that he was no closer to achieving his goal of true understanding.

One day his mentor died. After the funeral, he was filled with grief and sank into deep despair. In this grief, his soul left his body and soared above his head.

He saw his entire life and how foolish it was. He saw how he had wasted precious years studying books instead of living life.

He floated throughout the land and saw the world from the eyes of a bird. He realized how small everyone was from so high up. He realized how unimportant his fears and preoccupations were when compared to the whole of humanity.

When he returned to his body and told of his spiritual journey, he was revered as a wise man.

"I WATCHED MY OPERATION"

Anne-Marie, a thirty-three-year-old housewife, is a substitute teacher in an elementary school in a small town in upstate New York. Her husband is a clinical psychologist for a large national insurance company. When she was seven years old, she was hospitalized to have a tonsillectomy and to have an equalization tube placement to relieve an ear infection. During surgery, she was accidentally given too much general anesthesia by her anesthesiologist. She suddenly found herself out of the deep sleep of surgery and hovering above her own body on the operating table.

"I didn't know what was happening. I looked down on the operating table and saw five versions of myself as doctors tried to revive me. Three of the figures were real and two were negative images of myself. I tried to talk to the doctors, but no one was listening. They were just trying to get that body working again.

"Then the doctors settled down again when they got the heart started. I suddenly found my vision fading. When I awoke, I was back in my own body."

Anne-Marie's experience remains so vivid it seems as though it happened only yesterday. Whenever she lies down, the experience comes back to her. "Sometimes I have to jiggle myself to stay in my body," she says.

Oddly enough, these occasional out-of-body experiences help her gain perspective on difficult problems in her life. "They help me see the world from a different angle," she says, no pun intended.

"THERE WAS A CONTINUOUS RHYTHM"

Jim is a fifty-year-old supervisor at an aircraft manufacturing plant in Seattle, Washington. He has been married for thirty years and has two children. When he was six years old, he had a bout with scarlet fever that left him critically ill.

One night, as he labored for breath in his room, he felt as though he was slipping away from this life.

"Suddenly, I found myself in a long dark tube, with some strange and different music. There was a continuous rhythm that reminds me of sound you can hear when you place your ear against the mouth of a long pipe.

"I was just flying down this tunnel toward a light. There was something at the end of this tunnel, but I can't really say what it was. I could see my body zooming toward the Light so I know I was out of my body. I was convinced that I was dead, and I really wanted to get to the end of the tunnel to see what the next life held. But I never reached it, and I don't know why."

The experience had a profound effect upon Jim's life. He feels that it caused him to have a better relationship with both man and God. As he put it: "Even as a wild young man, I always had a strong desire to help others. The experience caused me to have compassion for others, especially those who face death. I have no fear of death, and it is my responsibility to help others who have that fear."

He feels that the experience brought him to God, even though he insists that this wasn't a religious experience for him. "I just know that there is something greater out there than us because I have experienced it. I realize that others have seen God when they have these experiences. I didn't. I only saw the Light, but that was enough for me."

"I WAS FILLED WITH CURIOSITY"

Here is another case of someone facing their maker as the result of a gas-siphoning accident. This sixty-four-year-old man's name is Bob, and his experience happened when he was six years old. He was siphoning gasoline out of a barrel at his family farm in Texas when he inhaled and swallowed a large amount. As he describes it, things happened fast:

"Suddenly, I was in a tunnel. At the end of the tunnel was something that looked like a portal, a doorway with a round top. It didn't feel as though I lost consciousness. In fact, I felt almost super-alive.

"I reached the end of the tunnel, and a hand reached out and pushed me away. It was my dead aunt. She smiled at me and said: 'No, Bobby, it's not your time.' The next thing I knew, I was floating about fifty feet above my body. I felt under my butt to see what I was sitting on and realized that I was sitting on nothing. I was truly floating!

"I watched a neighbor run up the road. All the way he was shouting 'Oh my God' until he reached my body. Then he began pushing on my chest until gasoline came out of my nose. Then—whoosh—I was back in my body."

This story has an interesting twist. Bob feels that this near-fatal event damaged his ability to concentrate and learn about a given subject. He felt that way until a couple of years ago when he turned thirty-seven. Then he "woke up," as he puts it, and when his supervisor gave him a set of blueprints to read as a joke, he discovered that he had the ability to read complex blueprints. Although Bob had only a seventh-grade education, had difficulty reading and was working as a laborer, he was able to read the blueprints as easily as an engineer.

Bob feels that his "awakening" was due to the near-death experience. Even though it happened more than thirty years before, the long-term effects of the NDE improved his mind.

I have trouble believing that such a distant event could suddenly give him newfound talent. There are a few examples of people who have demonstrated increased knowledge in mathematics and physics shortly after their experiences. For example, one adult with a high school education suddenly developed the ability to interpret the complex equations of nuclear physicists.

Even children demonstrate profound wisdom. Perhaps this wisdom or "great knowingness," as one child called it, comes from such an intense exposure to the Being of Light. I say that because the message from the Light is almost always one that encourages knowledge.

"I STEPPED BACK ACROSS"

Warren is a fifty-five-year-old construction worker with a wife and two children. When he was ten, he almost died from an allergic reaction to penicillin. As doctors began resuscitation, Warren lost consciousness. Then as he describes it:

> "Black clouds swirled all around me like I was in a heavy fog. Then suddenly, a point of light appeared. It moved closer and closer to me until the clouds suddenly cleared, and I was standing next to a narrow stream. I began to walk next to the stream until it got so narrow that I could step over it.
> "The other side of the stream was extremely peaceful. There were hills on the peaceful side that were lighted from behind and looked beautiful.

"As I walked, I was approached by an old man with a beard. I don't know for sure who he was, but I have the feeling he was one of my grandfathers. He stopped me and told me to go back across the stream. 'It's not your time,' he said.

"I turned and looked at the stream. It was quite wide at this point, but soon it narrowed. Then I stepped across and simply passed right into my body."

This experience has colored much of Warren's life. When union layoffs have left him without a job, for instance, the peace he felt on the other side of that stream returns to him. "Very little in life is worth getting upset about," he says.

"THERE SEEMED TO BE A BORDER"

Rick is twenty-five years old now, an age he almost didn't see thanks to meningitis, a bacterial infection of the brain. When he was five he became severely ill at home after surgery to remove a fungus from his head. His parents called an ambulance, but by the time it arrived, Rick was running a high temperature and was barely holding onto life. This is how he describes what happened to him:

"I remember leaving my physical body and seeing the transport team carrying me out of the house! I was following above them as they loaded my body into the ambulance.

"I didn't go with it. Instead I briefly went into my sister's head and saw the world through her eyes.

Then I saw my father weeping as he got into the car to take the family to the hospital. He was sure I was going to die, and I felt sorry that my possible death was causing him this kind of pain.

"I went ahead to the hospital to see what kind of room I was going to get. I saw a girl who was about twelve years old in the room that I was supposed to go into. Since I was so sick, they decided to move her and give me the room alone.

"I then left the earth and traveled down a long tunnel. I came to a bright opening and passed through it. Out in the brightness I was engulfed by fog. There seemed to be a border, something like a waterline on the beach that separated me from the true Light. I knew that if I entered the Light, I would not return to my body. The Light was all love, all knowing, and the sky was warm and friendly. I was trying to decide whether I should go into the Light or not when I just returned to my body."

This experience amazed Rick's family because of the rich details it provided about events going on around him. Since Rick's body was in the ambulance speeding toward the hospital, an out-of-body experience would have been necessary for him to see his father crying in the family car behind him. Leaving his body and traveling ahead of the ambulance would have been necessary for him to see the twelve-year-old girl being transferred from his room before he arrived at the hospital. The fact that he was comatose before leaving for the hospital and for several days thereafter makes his experience even more baffling.

Rick's NDE left him with two strong beliefs. One

is that life is precious, but death is nothing to be feared. The other is that we are all born with the knowledge we need to solve life's problems. "The answers are all inside," he says. "If we can just climb over our egos."

"THERE WERE THINGS I HAD TO DO BEFORE ENTERING THE LIGHT"

At the age of ten, Paul ran into his kitchen and slipped on a wet floor. He landed on his stomach so hard that he ruptured his spleen. According to his medical records, he swelled with fluids and went into shock from internal bleeding. His parents rushed him to the hospital, where his heart stopped. This is what he experienced:

"I left my body, although I still felt like I was connected to it by a string. I floated up to a corner of the room and watched as three doctors worked frantically to rescue me. I was sure I was going to die, and I have to admit that I found their efforts to save me kind of funny.

"I then went down a long tunnel and approached a warm light. At the other end of the tunnel, I was met by a being who talked to me. I thought of him as a greeter then, and that is what I still call him. He was a greeter.

"The greeter was not in a physical form. Rather, he was more a feeling or an awareness. He told me that I could not stay in the tunnel, that I had to either go back or continue on. If I continued, there would be no return.

"I didn't make an actual decision to return, but I did get an idea from the greeter that there was purpose to my life.

"While I was thinking about whether to stay or return, I felt myself enter my body. I was about the size of a BB when I went into my body. Then I expanded and filled up all the space.

"For a while I longed for that light. Then I realized that someday I would see it again. In the meantime, I had things to do."

The feeling that there is a purpose to life is one of the results of many childhood NDEs. Much as the near-death experience itself, that purpose may have meaning only to the person who receives the message.

Rick's purpose was family. He believes that he was made to live because he was to have a loving relationship with his family, especially his autistic son.

"For some reason, someone thought that it was important that I have a family and nourish it," says Rick. "I am sure that is the reason I was left here on earth."

"I WAS TRAVELING AT A TREMENDOUS SPEED"

When Ed was only five years old, he released the emergency brake on the family car and became trapped in the car door as it rolled down their steep driveway and into the road. His father dug him out from under the left rear tire and began giving him mouth-to-mouth resuscitation. His mother ran down the hill with the car keys and the parents began a fran-

tic race to the hospital to save their son. Ed describes
what happened next:

"I saw myself sitting between my parents as
though I was outside the front window and looking
in. I could see everything. My parents had panic on
their faces and both of them were crying. My face
was bruised and battered, and it looked as though
every single blood vessel had burst.

"How long I was outside the car I don't know.
But suddenly, I began to float up and then everything became dark. Then I felt like I was speeding
up. Soon I was traveling at a tremendous speed in
total darkness. It was like I imagine space travel to
be.

"Suddenly I felt like I was standing on a loading
dock with a very powerful and bright light hanging
over my head. This light was very bright and filled
with love and knowledge. I was there with a man,
but I couldn't see him clearly because of the bright
light. Thoughts were coming into my mind from the
bright light. I felt a loving God and love for people
in general. There were also beautiful music and vo-
cals like a choir that I couldn't quite understand."

It became clear from Ed's first few days out of the
hospital that the experience had transformed him. The
first sign came at church, when the preacher was talking about a "fearful and terrible God." This disturbed
Ed. He told his mother that he didn't want to attend
church anymore.

In grade school, he spoke frequently about the need
to love one another. When pressed, he would tell
teachers and classmates about the time he saw God.

This led to problems in class, and eventually, he was sent to school psychologists, who told him that he had too vivid an imagination.

In college, he studied philosophy of religion and learned techniques for meditation. Sometimes, when deep in meditation, he can see the Light again. Those moments are bliss, says Ed, because he can reexperience the event that led to his faith.

Over the years, Ed has been the target of a great deal of ridicule for talking openly about his near-death experience and the philosophy of life it gave him. For years, he was hurt by the callous reactions of people. Now after hearing about the experiences of others who have had NDEs, he realizes that most people ridicule him because they have never had such a powerful and transformative experience. "It's a relief to finally come to that conclusion," he told me. "I feel lucky to have had the experience. Unfortunately, so many of us require many years just to incorporate the experience into our lives. I used to feel hurt when people made fun of me for seeing 'a light.' Now I'm understanding. After all, if they haven't had such an experience, how can I expect them to understand what I am talking about?"

"I BEGGED GOD TO LET ME DIE"

Sam is a sixty-year-old insurance company executive with a wife and two children. At the age of seventeen, he had a near-death experience on a battlefield in the Pacific. As he describes it, he was shot several times while lying in a foxhole. Several soldiers around him were killed, and he was bleeding profusely from his wounds. "I was in a great amount of pain," he told me. "Several times I begged God to let me die." Instead, something else happened. Sam describes it:

> "I must have passed out from blood loss. I remember just staring at the sky and hearing bullets and the other sounds of combat when everything went black, and there was no sound. I don't know how long I was in this blacked-out state, but I began to rise out of my body. I felt no pain as I just seemed to stand up right there on the battlefield. Ahead of me was a beautiful light that took away my pain. It was shining and beautiful, and I could just stand there on this horrible battlefield and be safe with it."

Medics came and took Sam to surgery. He was then shipped back to the States.

Sam says that a taste of the experience comes back to him occasionally. When he is in periods of severe stress or pain, he feels the presence of the Light and is able to feel peace.

At one time, Sam was so curious about his experience that he went to a psychotherapist to try and relive it through hypnosis. He was unable to do so, breaking out of the trance before seeing the Light. "The experience happens when I need it, not when I want it," says Sam.

"I WANTED TO TELL HIM I WAS ALL RIGHT"

At the age of fifteen, Cindy became very ill with mononucleosis. When the disease began to affect her heart, Cindy was hospitalized. While there, she experienced what might have been a cardiac arrest. She tells what happened next:

> "Suddenly, I was floating over my body, and I saw my father holding my hand down below. He was very concerned as the doctors and nurses worked on me. I wanted to tell him I was all right and that I was very warm and comfortable where I was. It was very dark around me, and my body was illuminated by the Light.
> "I saw the concern on my father's face and decided that I had to return to my body."

Cindy is now forty-four. She feels that her near-death experience made her more tolerant of other people's beliefs. She also believes in reincarnation, but not in God. "For me this experience proved that there is life immediately after death," said Cindy. "My experience didn't show me a God, so I can't really believe in one."

TRANSFORMED AFTER ATTEMPTED SUICIDE: TWO CASE STUDIES

Case Study #1: "Care for Yourself"

Beverly is a happily married, forty-seven-year-old woman who is quick to say that she is glad to be alive.

She seems so happy to me now that it is hard to believe that as a child she almost succeeded in killing herself.

She was raised in Philadelphia by parents who were so abusive that she is still unable to discuss the specifics of her childhood. How she attempted to commit suicide makes me believe that life for her was indeed horrific.

At the age of seven, she towed her sled to the top of a very steep hill and aimed it at a cement bench by the street. Her plan was to slide headfirst into the bench. Without hesitating, she lay down and took what was to be her last ride.

She successfully hit the bench and immediately found herself floating above her body. She saw children surrounding her, but no one went for help. Instead, they examined the wound and went back to their play. This heartless reaction didn't surprise her because she lived in a tough, inner-city neighborhood.

She floated higher and higher to the rooftops of the buildings, where she had never been before. She also saw that the apartments had fake Tudor fronts. Things then changed:

"I went up and up and faded into a deep silver-blue surrounding. Then came something that looked like a big umbrella without a stick. This umbrella seemed to fold around me, and everything became very dark. Then, suddenly, I was in a very intense, bright light. I felt warm and loved in a way that I had never felt before.

"Then I heard a voice from the Light: 'You have

made a mistake. Your life is not yours to take. You must go back.' I argued with the voice. 'No one cares about me.' The answer I got back was shocking. 'You're right. No one on this planet cares about you, including your parents. It is your job to care for yourself.' "

Beverly was suddenly returned to her body, which at this point wasn't a pleasant place to be. She was in intense pain. Her mouth had been imbedded in a wooden railing around the bench. Her neck was broken. She tried to move her head and lost many of her teeth and a piece of her tongue.

Beverly remembers thinking that as soon as she could she would go back to the top of the snowy hill and try to kill herself again. As soon as that thought came to mind, Beverly was engulfed by the umbrella and taken out of her body again.

Warm in this "bubble of love and life," she was treated to an awesome vision. The warm bubble melted the snow and ice from a nearby tree on which she often played. The bubble showed her that, although the tree was encased in snow and ice now, it would have green leaves on it in the summertime. She saw herself sitting beneath the tree, eating a sweet apple from its branches, and feeling pleasure and joy. Suddenly, she understood what was being shown to her.

"I saw that the winter tree with the snow on it and the summer tree with the apples were two parts of a whole. I saw that my life now was like the winter tree. And when I realized that summer was ahead, I was willing to go back into my body."

Life was not easy for this woman, who had a long recovery process. She spent many months in a coma and still has some paralysis in her fingers. As she says, "It wasn't as tough to get out of my body as it has been to get back in."

The experience immediately transformed her. After her coma, she spoke up more for her rights, becoming a self-advocate instead of a dispirited victim of child abuse.

She has spent her life establishing a family of love, the type that she never had herself. She is happily married with three children. She wears an umbrella on a charm necklace to always remember what the experience taught her: "When you hurt yourself, everything is hurt."

Case Study #2: "You'll Have to Stick Around"

At the age of eleven, James swallowed handfuls of Darvon, codeine, Tylenol, and aspirin and walked into a wooded park to die. Fortunately, a couple of young lovers followed his path about an hour later and found his comatose body. They called an ambulance. James was rescued with almost no time to spare.

When he was revived, he told of an experience of light, the same experience he told me about nearly twenty years after it happened.

"Everything went dark when I died, just as I thought it would. Then suddenly my world was filled with light. It seemed to fill in all the dark spots in my life, namely, those feelings of emptiness that I had from being an abused child.

"A spirit in the Light asked me why I tried to kill myself. So I told him about how bad my life and world were. He was kind but not very sympathetic. He said, 'Well, you'll just have to stick around and see what you can do with your life.' "

James has done wonderful things with his life. Although his conversation with the Light made him think he was insane for years afterward, he now realizes that he gained new purpose through his experience.

At the age of twenty-five, James works in the nation's only summer camp for children with AIDS. He now considers himself lucky. "My near-death experience taught me that I had to create my own possibilities. I never would have found that out on my own."

DIDN'T KNOW HE HAD DIED

I feel honored to have heard these transformative NDEs from two survivors of childhood suicide attempts. Childhood suicide attempts are rare and usually predicts a lifetime of mental instability. Yet here are two successful adults who have conquered their childhood traumas and now live extraordinary lives.

Usually, the adult describing a childhood NDE is similar to a child telling the experience themselves. The patients are fairly casual, and the actual telling is very brief. The childhood experience remains pure and simple, a vivid memory that persists and influences the rest of a person's life. These experiencers are calm about death and animated about life. As one man told me: "It left me with an open mind but no other real effects."

This is a very important finding. The mind does not alter the childhood NDE over time, nor does the experiencer change or embellish the story after years of retelling the event.

It is interesting to note that adults presenting their childhood NDEs sometimes don't think they had an NDE. They often start by saying, "Gee, I guess this wasn't really a near-death experience, but here's what happened to me." Later, when we review their cases, their medical records confirm that they have indeed had such an experience.

After giving a talk on NDEs to the staff at my local hospital, one of the emergency room physicians claimed that these experiences weren't spiritual, but drug related.

"I've never really had a near-fatal experience, but I know for a fact that anesthetic agents can cause exactly the kind of experience you are describing. These NDEs aren't unusual at all and are certainly caused by drugs."

I had carefully examined the effects of commonly used anesthetic agents in my own work and had found that they didn't cause NDEs. I asked him about his proof.

"I had such an experience when I was a child," he said. "I had a routine tonsillectomy at the age of six, and I floated out of my body. I saw the doctors working on me, and I saw a bright light. I felt like I was with God and I felt his love. Then I was sucked back into my body.''

I was curious. I asked him to research his medical records to see what anesthetic agents had been used. To his great surprise, he found that his heart had stopped briefly during surgery. There was also a notation that his parents had not been informed because his heart had stopped for such a brief period of time.

He did not recognize it for what it was.

CAME BACK FOR A PURPOSE—LOVE

Experiencing the Light has given people new purpose in life. By that, I don't mean that they were saved by God to invent a cure for cancer or to save the world from nuclear destruction. Nothing that grandiose.

Their purpose is quite simple and can be easily summed up: revere life and see the intricate connections throughout the universe.

Even many years after their NDEs, these special people believe that the Light gave them the power to transform their lives. In many ways, NDEers have become so transformed that they have given up some involvement with their own egos. This process has enabled some to become much more sensitive to others.

One woman, for instance, told me that her NDE gave her the ''power to read minds.'' By that, she didn't mean that she could read them like a book. ''I have just become very intuitive and can understand how others think. This has helped me in my job as a nurse." Many children and adults have said that NDEs make them more sensitive to people around them.

The messages given to these children of the Light are not new or controversial. They are as old as mankind itself and have served as the primary fuel of our great religions:

"Love your neighbor and cherish life."

"Do unto others as you would have them do unto you."

"Clean up your own mess."

"Be the best that you can be."

"Contribute to society."

"Be nice, kind, and loving."

These messages have a special urgency for those who have had near-death experiences. Why? Perhaps since the messages came to them at the point of death, they must be important.

8

The Seattle Study Revisited

Knowledge by suffering entereth; And Life is perfected by Death.

—*Elizabeth Barrett Browning*

After eight years of scientific research into near-death experiences in children, I decided to reinterview the original group of patients from the Seattle study. When I first spoke to them, they had never before shared their entire experience.

Back then they were shy and sometimes reluctant to talk about "floating on air" or about a "man who glowed like a light bulb." Sometimes the only way I could get them to speak about their NDEs would be to hand them paper and crayons and let them draw a picture of it.

Now, almost ten years later, I wondered what these kids would be like. Had they adjusted well with their peers? Were they ahead of their classes academically? Did they have a perspective on the world that differed from their friends? Or did their profound spiritual experience make no difference at all?

I found that these children have become special teenagers who have excellent relationships with their families. They share a maturity and wisdom that is humbling.

This group from the Seattle study displays a conspicuous absence of drug abuse and even experimentation. They exhibit little rebellion against authority, no excessive risk taking, and no teenage pregnancies. These people were selected for the study because they had survived cardiac arrest. Yet instead of the brain damage and retardation that usually result from such a traumatic event, they had good grades and fine behavior.

I spoke to each and every child from the original study and found these traits in all of them. Here is some of what I discovered when I visited these special kids.

PATIENT ONE: "MORE SERIOUS . . . A LOT HAPPIER"

For instance, Patient One in my study is now twenty years old and vividly remembers his experience. He left his body when his heart stopped and watched as physicians worked frantically to save him. His experience had been impressive to me because of the wealth of detail he was able to remember from his own resuscitation. Everything he described was entirely accurate, including snatches of conversation, precise details of how a jelly was applied to his body, how physicians cleared others from the metal bed before pushing the buttons on the cardioversion paddles, and how his clothing was cut with scissors to expose his arms, legs, and chest.

His experience had been so authentic that it is hard to explain unless he actually was on the ceiling watching his own resuscitation.

Patient One does not see his near-death experience as a religious one. He doesn't even see it as proof of life after death. He didn't even know he'd had an NDE until he heard me talking about them on a radio show. Yet still this experience has had a deep effect upon the way he thinks and lives.

He describes himself as being "more serious than most kids my age, but a lot happier." He feels that he understands the meaning of life and what his purpose is, even though he cannot put it into words: "I developed diabetes as a teenager, and my experience helped me deal with that. It kept me from being discouraged, and it made me aware of how precious life is."

His philosophy of life is simple and serene. He has a vision of what he wants to do and is working hard to achieve it. He wants to get married and have a family, and he wants to work in a trade that he can count on for work.

He ended our conversation with virtually the identical words of so many other children of the Light: "I know one thing. I am not afraid to die. My near-death experience has made me more aware of life. It has kept me from being interested in drugs or driving around in cars and getting high like my friends do.''

PATIENT SIX: "I FEEL CALMER AND MORE IN CONTROL"

Michelle (patient six in the Seattle study) was the eight-year-old who nearly died of a diabetic coma. She left her body and was able to identify accurately many details of her resuscitation. Then she saw a box in front of her with a red and a green button.

Behind her stood tall beings in white that she later called doctors. Although they coaxed her to push the red button, she chose the green instead and returned to her body.

Although she called these beings doctors, they glowed from an inner light and had the same characteristics that other children describe in angels. Michelle also had to make a decision about crossing a barrier, which in her case was choosing the correct button. All of these were clearly the NDE's core experience.

How did this NDE effect Michelle? She says that it caused her to "see life differently than most people. Little things that bother others don't really bother me. I feel calmer and more in control."

Michelle sees her NDE as "a special happening." She is a vegetarian because she doesn't want to do anything that might hurt animals. She has a deep belief in God, but does not attend church on a regular basis.

Michelle's mother calls her "serene" and "very mature for her age." And as with the others in the study, Michelle doesn't fear death, but wants to make sure that she lives life to the fullest.

PATIENT THREE: "CAN'T YOU FEEL IT?"

Dean (patient three in the study) has now had a second near-death experience as a result of his chronic kidney problems.

Dean's two NDEs coupled with his chronic kidney problems helped him put his life into perspective. Once the rebel of the family, Dean has now embraced his family's faith in Christ, becoming a devout Christian.

His transformation has helped his family deal with the incredible strain of raising children with kidney problems. Dean's younger brother died of kidney failure, and to stay alive he and his sister spend twelve to eighteen hours a week attached to a home dialysis machine. The divorce rate in such situations is well over seventy-five percent. Yet this family, for all intents and purposes, leads a fairly normal life.

Have Dean's NDEs helped them achieve that normalcy? "These things have helped me gain comfort through God," Dean said. "Can't you feel it? The spirit is everywhere in this house."

I have to admit that I did feel a rare spirit of family and a joy with these fine people.

These children have grown up to become remarkable teenagers. Not rocket scientists, not high priests in robes, just positive and upbeat kids with a joy that is inspiring. They have not become involved with drugs or alcohol. They have not gotten pregnant and they rarely—according to their parents—get out of line.

Their actions speak louder than words about the reality of the near-death experience.

A TRANSFORMATION FOR ME, TOO

And how has a decade of near-death research affected me and the way I approach medicine? It has changed everything in my life, including my views on medicine, the way I see society, and even the way I deal with my family.

When I began my studies eight years ago, I was in mainstream medicine. I laughingly referred to myself as a "rodent brain surgeon" who researched the effects of radiation therapy on a child's brain.

I undertook near-death studies as a sideline to an already busy schedule. I was fascinated by the subject, but always felt that we would demonstrate that a particular drug or disease process was responsible for this phenomenon. When I accepted Dr. Raymond Moody's challenge to study NDEs scientifically, I felt certain that science would explain them.

All these years later, I accept what the ancients knew: All men must die and death is not to be feared. There is a Light that we will all experience after death, and that Light represents joy, peace, and unconditional love.

These children have taught me that we each have

the ability to experience the Light and that the Light teaches us that we are each important in our own way.

Our research brought together new and preexisting information that revealed a genetically imprinted circuit in the brain that can generate the near-death experience. The existence of that area has caused me to include the concept of the soul in my medical thinking. Why? The simplest, most logical way to explain our current knowledge of man's consciousness is the hypothesis that there is actually a soul within each of us, independent of brain tissue.

I have reexamined a generation of scientific research into higher brain function and have found that the soul hypothesis explains many "unexplained" events. It explains out-of-body experiences, the sensation of leaving the body and accurately describing details outside of the body's field of view. Events such as floating out of the physical body and giving accurate details of one's own cardiac arrest—things a person couldn't see even if their eyes were open—are virtually impossible to explain if we do not believe in a consciousness separate from our bodies that could be called a soul.

I have documented that we have an area in the brain, the right temporal lobe, that some researchers describe as the seat of the soul. It is connected to the hippocampus, which serves as the brain's master control, sorting out thousands of pieces of sensory input and deciding which of them should be acted upon.

It contains our unconscious desires and our ability to dream. Without this area, we would be like robots, unable to initiate purposeful activity and not caring about the passage of time.

The hippocampus has been called "the man in the machine" by some neurologists. It is directly connected to areas in the right temporal and occipital lobes that contain the neuronal circuitry to create near-death experiences. The collapse of the visual fields to create the tunnel experience occurs in the occipital lobes. The sensations of leaving the body, seeing dead relatives, hearing heavenly music, speaking with God, and reviewing one's own life are part of our genetic makeup, "hard-wired" into each of us.

Right now, science does not attempt to explain NDEs. It relies instead on vague allusions to "endorphins at the point of death," as if that could somehow explain everything. The problem is that science tries to explain all mysterious brain activity with current catchphrases, endorphins, and other neurotransmitters.

The near-death experience is the first psychological experience to be located within the brain. Others soon will follow. Several excellent research studies document the effects of emotions upon disease. For example, if an anesthesiologist whispers "You will get well soon" in the ear of a patient during surgery, that patient will leave the hospital an average of two days sooner than a control group that has not been given such tender loving words. This is fact. Such information is not routinely used in surgery because surgeons tend to reject the psychological. If such words were pills, they would be ordering thousands of them.

By locating the area for NDEs within the brain, we have anatomy to back up the psychological experience. *We know where the circuit board is*. Now neurologists can accept the spirituality of the NDE because we know where they are generated within our brains. This acceptance is important. Since medical professionals deal with people in spiritual as well as physical crisis, it is important for them to be able to accept and explain a wide variety of phenomena not found in most medical textbooks.

Near-death experiences are an example of a psychological experience that can be anatomically located within the brain. Since they are often profound and mystical experiences, the study of NDEs will help to reunite the centuries-old split of science and spirit. I once heard a minister preach that a small piece of God is in every one of us. I thought to myself: "God is in each and every one of us, and the ability to perceive God is located in the right temporal lobe, within the Sylvian fissure." I do not think that my anatomical restatement of his message detracted in any way from it.

There are many examples of psychological experiences that have been found to be located in specific areas in the brain. Specific areas in our limbic systems, an ancient area of the brain located deep within the cortex, code for the emotions of rage and anger. The same hormones which generate these emotions have been found to have specific effects on our immune systems. Endocrinologists will soon be able to describe the exact biochemical pathways by which anger and rage lead to increased infections and cancer.

Dr. Vernon Neppe, the director of the Division of Neuropsychiatry at the University of Washington, has documented that experiences such as *déjà vu* experiences and precognitive dreams and intuitions are also located within the temporal lobe. He agrees that the value of these experiences is to recognize that an experience such as *déjà vu*, which the majority of human beings will have at some point in their lifetime, is therefore a natural and normal experience, and not paranormal at all. He describes a patient who thought that she was crazy because she occasionally saw halos of light around certain friends, and had precognitive dreams which seemed to come true. He feels that he prevented her from having a psychotic breakdown by simply reassuring her that these experiences are common and normal, and were not, in her case, symptoms of being crazy.

Physicians often ignore well-documented proof of the effects of the mind on the body. Several studies have shown the value of simply talking to patients before surgery about post-operative pain and the normal healing process. These patients are sent home an average of two days earlier than patients who do not receive this treatment for the mind. Many studies show that making positive statements about how well the patient is doing and how quickly they will heal in the operating room will result in a decreased need for pain medications and an earlier discharge date. If I were to market a pill to surgeons that would result in less post-

operative pain and a faster surgical recovery, I would
be selling them in dump-truck loads. A pill that heals
is far more acceptable than words that can have the
same effect.

The real value of my research team's results is that
we have established that the near-death experience is
a natural and normal event that happens to human beings when they die. They are not obscure psychic phenomena to be lumped together with UFO sightings
and Bigfoot. The understanding of how emotions can
effect our ability to fight disease, or how mentally preparing a patient for surgery can lead to faster post-
operative healing, will be made easier once we change
our perception of how the mind and body interrelate.
For medical scientists, the anatomical localization of
an out-of-body experience to the temporal lobe makes
NDEs more understandable and study of these experiences more respectable. I predict that twenty years
from now many such psychological processes will be
anatomically localized within the brain, and that we
will see a reintegration of man's spirit with his tech-
nological genius.

When I present the anatomical location of near-death
experiences at various talks and lectures, I am often
told by those who have had these experiences that they
resent my attempts to localize NDEs in the brain. To
them, attempting to scientifically explain these events
is the same as attempting to debunk them, to imply
that they are not real.

Near-death experiences do not need science to prove
that they are real. Whether or not there is some part

of man that can leave the physical body is for each person to decide for himself. The fact that science cannot measure the soul in the laboratory does not mean that it does not exist.

One of the nurses at Valley General Hospital told me of her grandmother who had a near-death experience after surviving a heart attack. Andriette's grandmother told her that she had been to heaven, and was no longer afraid to die. Andriette asked me if I thought that the fact that children had NDEs was proof that there is life after death. She was searching for reassurance that her grandmother had in fact seen heaven. I told her that I have agonized over that very question, and have concluded that science cannot answer it.

Several weeks later she told me that her grandmother had had a second heart attack, and had been resuscitated, but was being kept alive by life-support machines. She asked her grandmother if she had returned to heaven, after the second attack. Her grandmother nodded her head to indicate "yes." Andriette then asked her grandmother if she was afraid to die, and she shook her head "no." Her grandmother then peacefully died with a look of joy on her face.

I asked Andriette if she now believed that her grandmother had truly gone to heaven, and she said, "Well, my grandmother believed she did, and that is [proof] enough for me." Like Andriette, I also believe in the reality of the near-death experience. The effects that such events have on the lives (and deaths) of those who have them are "proof enough" for me.

My research team has documented the transformative power of NDEs in the people who have them. These transformations are healthy ones, emphasizing a joy and devotion to life. One person told me that her experience taught her that ''grief is growth.'' Another person learned that everything in the world is interconnected and that whatever problems one faces, there is a reason for that problem. The knowledge that a loving bright light awaits us all at the point of death seems to generate an excitement and dedication to living life to its fullest before joining that light.

FERTILE AREA FOR RESEARCH

Psychologist Carl Jung felt that therapy and psychoanalysis rarely change one's life. Changes only occur, said Jung, through experiences such as a mystical conversion.

Near-death experiences certainly represent such a conversion. Their ability to transform should not be ignored. Because of their mystical qualities, NDEs are often dismissed by physicians who feel a need to quantify everything. Research into the transformative qualities of the near-death experience could have a tremendous impact upon our health-care system.

Perhaps a joint effort by neurochemists and psychiatrists could be initiated to learn other ways of accessing this area of the brain. Many of our health problems have roots in the mind, such as alcoholism, drug addiction, and obesity. Alcoholism is virtually untreatable by medication, psychiatry, or behavioral control.

Imagine if the transformative reaction to NDEs could be available to anyone who wants the power to change his life for the better.

OTHER RESEARCH POSSIBILITIES

Another possibility for near-death research would be through blood analysis. Since we know that a large number of people having cardiac arrests will have near-death experiences, why not draw some extra blood from them for analysis? These patients have a considerable amount of blood drawn anyway. It would be easy and ethical to draw an extra tube to analyze for evidence of which, if any, of sixty neuropeptides might be involved in triggering NDEs. We could also examine this blood for elevated levels of serotonin and endorphins.

This information could then be used to design new drugs that could activate the areas of the brain responsible for this transformation.

Such an experiment would be a joint effort between psychiatrists, who could collect and quantify the clinical data; neurologists, who could identify specific areas of brain function; and neurochemists, who could design ways of biochemically marking neurochemical activity.

Another research project could utilize specialized EEGs to document the activity of the hippocampus. These EEGs read the P-300 brain wave, which can tell such remarkable things as a person's leadership abilities, likelihood of becoming an alcoholic, or ability to pay attention to the world.

Since patients who have had NDEs often report that the world looks fresh and new, their P-300 brain waves could be compared with those of the general population to discover any difference.

The brain waves of NDEers could also be compared with people who report ecstatic states and out-of-body experiences through meditation in order to see if there are any similarities.

In a more basic realm, few studies currently exist in the medical literature to document the psychological effects of simply discussing death and dying with terminal patients and their families. Isn't that a shocking commentary on how far we have fallen from the time-honored deathbed scene in which the dying person was in control? Not only are most dying patients completely dependent on physicians and nurses for their every need, but we have them in a position of psychological dependence.

By discussing predeath visions, near-death experiences, and death itself with dying patients and their families, we can take grief out of isolation and stop ignoring this difficult yet inevitable event. By discussing the dying process, we will learn to heal ourselves, families will learn from the grieving process, and physicians and nurses will prevent the burnout of working with the dying. This is strictly my opinion. No data exists to support or deny that opinion.

Many other research opportunities exist, all of them valuable in advancing medicine:

- We need to survey the attitudes that nurses and physicians have about life and death. Knowing these belief systems would help us understand how the attitudes of the care-givers can influence what the patients are willing to share with them.
- Do the predeath visions or near-death experiences of a dying patient help the surviving spouses or parents deal with their grief? These events may offer valuable opportunities to resolve grief that are being ignored.
- It is well known that widows and widowers often die within one year of the death of their spouse. Can aggressive intervention with a discussion of near-death experiences decrease this mortality rate? One family told me that when their son died a minister told them: "Your son is alright. He is in heaven now. I know because I have been there myself." He then told them of his own NDE. It proved to be a great relief to the family.
- Does this type of counseling help or hurt those who are grieving? No studies currently exist to let us know.
- Do open discussions of predeath visions help to prevent physician and nurse burnout in intensive care units and on wards with high mortality rates?

Dr. Karen Ollness, professor of pediatrics at Rainbow Babies' Hospital in Cleveland, told me of an innovative program she started at Milwaukee Children's Hospital. The hospital staff held weekly meetings to discuss ways in which reverence for the human spirit could be integrated into the hospital routine. This informal weekly workshop became very popular and has had an impact on the entire hospital.

For example, seminars on death and dying are held for the housekeepers and janitorial staff in an effort to create a total climate for the healing process. When a patient dies, the hospital staff routinely attends memorial services and funerals. These practices help care-givers cope with the loss of a patient.

These support groups and procedures would be easy to duplicate in hospitals around the country. All it takes is a few people willing to talk about these subjects in a loving and open manner.

- Does counseling about near-death experiences in terminally ill patients in hospitals or in hospices create a better environment for them? Do they require as many drugs? Does helping patients die in control and with dignity, including a deathbed scene in which they are coherent and not heavily sedated, heal the grief of surviving family members? Studies need to be done to find these answers.
- Are there ways to encourage patients to have pre-death visions? For instance, can hypnosis help the patient have a therapeutic predeath vision?

This isn't as peculiar as it might seem. Dr. G. G. Gardner, a psychologist at the University of Colorado Children's Hospital, actually accomplished this with a patient she calls David.

This thirteen-year-old boy was dying of leukemia. Dr. Gardner became involved when she was asked to teach David self-hypnosis in an effort to control his painful vomiting and retching. She did so with great success. Soon David and the rest of his family wanted to know other ways they could use hypnosis. David was so enthralled with the process that he even tried to hypnotize the family dog.

When it became clear that David had only a few months to live, Dr. Gardner asked him to think of an image or symbol that could help him deal with the anxiety of death. David chose an eagle, which could soar through the air—away from his pain-filled body—to a place of peace and love. His family used this image to prepare him for death. In the final days of his life, his father would whisper, "Soar, David, go to that special place."

He died in his father's arms, flying from his pain one last time.

David's image of the soaring eagle was an archetype that arose from his unconscious during hypnosis. The types of predeath vision I presented earlier have been of a very different nature: visions of heaven or spirit guides that arise spontaneously, not out of guided meditations.

I predict that any person who is willing to listen to a dying patient will hear that patient speak of a vision that has the power to heal. They may speak of an eagle soaring to a private and secure place. They may speak of a land of *déjà vu* where they can experience the pleasures of sex (as one of my teenage patients did), or they may speak of a wonderful summerland in which there is a crystal castle.

These visions are real to the person having them

and shouldn't be treated as examples of "disorientation" or "confusion." Words like these lead physicians to medicate the visions right out of a dying patient.

It has been well documented that as a patient approaches death he becomes more and more isolated from family and medical team. Physicians actually spend less time at their bedside. Family members visit less frequently and for shorter periods of time. Once the diagnosis of a fatal illness is made, there is a dramatic decrease in visits, phone calls, and nurse or physician time.

Can education and counseling about near-death experiences reverse this pattern and give the dying patient support when they most need it? Maybe. Let's study the question and find out.

LESSONS IN COMPASSION

There is one important lesson I have learned from a decade of near-death studies: Listen, be compassionate, and understand that people—including children—have a need to feel in control.

This lesson has been brought home to me many times, including once by Mr. Rogers. This popular star of television's *Mr. Rogers' Neighborhood* came to Children's Hospital and shared many stories of how listening to children gives them control over their own healing processes.

Mr. Rogers told of one girl who was in a total body cast as a result of multiple injuries sustained in an automobile accident. She could not move her arms or legs and had to spend her days staring at the ceiling.

She became deeply depressed and refused to eat. Then "a kind and sensitive person" thought of giving her a New Year's Eve party favor that whistled and unrolled when blown. The girl loved this toy and soon drove the staff pleasantly crazy with the endless sounds of the noisemaker.

This newfound sense of control helped her regain her appetite and speed her healing process.

Another young patient was forced to have strict bedrest for rheumatic fever. She became severely depressed and refused to allow doctors to examine her or to draw the necessary blood samples.

Once again, "a kind and thoughtful person" did an unorthodox thing: He gave her a water pistol. Now, when the doctors and technicians came into the room, they had to be shot with water before they could stick her with a needle. Once again, control; the type that can only work when such powerful figures as doctors are willing to be shot with a stream of water.

Once we physicians start listening to patients and respecting and sharing with them, they will give us extra tools to help in the healing process.

Let me give an example of another healing vision from my own practice. Upon learning of my interest in near-death experiences, a patient shared with me a vision she had about her son who died at age ten.

When he was six months old, she found out that he had cerebral palsy. She was informed of this diagnosis in a horrible way. After an extensive series of tests at a large city hospital, a nurse approached her and said, "Has anyone told you yet?" She replied, "No, what do you mean?" The nurse simply handed her a piece of paper with "cerebral palsy" written on it.

She was distraught. She received no counseling, no compassionate shoulder to cry on, just the words "cerebral palsy" written on a piece of paper.

That night she saw a vision of her son at the age of ten. He was smiling, beautiful, and healthy and seemed to be saying to her, "Look, Mom, I'm all right." She clung to the memory of that vision throughout her life. Although he could not eat, speak, sit up, or walk, she continued to see him as happy and well as he had appeared that one mystical night.

At the age of ten, he died in his sleep. It was then that she realized the meaning of her vision: He was free of a body crippled by cerebral palsy.

She didn't come to me asking if I believed in life after death or if I thought her son was happy now. The vision had answered both of those questions for her. All she needed was comfort and assurance that what happened was "meant to be."

Why she had a premonition of what was "meant to be," I do not know. Perhaps it all comes down to the words of psychotherapist Carl Jung, who said: "We should not pretend to understand the world only by the intellect; we comprehend it just as much by feeling. Therefore the judgement of the intellect is, at best, only the half of the truth."

After ten years of listening to the near-death experiences of children, I find myself agreeing with Jung:

Science—as great as it is—tells only half the story about life beyond and the human soul. The children of the Light tell the rest.

Listen to what they have told me:

"I have a wonderful secret to tell you. I have been climbing a staircase to heaven."

"I just wanted to get to that Light. Forget my body, forget everything. I just wanted to get to that Light."

"There were a lot of good things in that Light."

"I was told that life is painful and that I had to go back anyway."

"I heard a voice say, 'Go back, Bobby. You have a job to do.'"

"There was a beautiful Light that had everything good in it. For about a week, I could see sparkles of that Light in everything."

"Before falling asleep at night, I could see that Light."

"I wasn't afraid to live again because I knew that someday I would be with that Light."

"When you hurt yourself, everything is hurt."

"You'll see. Heaven is fun."

Appendix

Why They Aren't NDEs

Some skeptics claim that near-death experiences are hallucinations resulting from a variety of drugs, psychological phenomena, or physiological stress.

To offer a balanced viewpoint, I am presenting these drugs and other phenomena that the debunkers claim can cause NDE-like experiences and a synopsis of the medical research showing what each does.

As you will be able to see from the scientific research, none of these mimics the powerful experiences revealed in this book.

Lysergic Acid (LSD): LSD, a drug that was popular in the sixties, is a crystalline form of acid known to cause hallucinations. LSD frequently causes a sensation of leaving the physical body and often leaves one with the feeling of having had a religious experience. LSD has inconsistent traits, but basically, it causes distortions of body image, visual hallucinations of colors and patterns, and a variety of bizarre emotions and images. NDEs have a consistent core experience of leaving the physical body and traveling up a tunnel that is not experienced by those who take LSD.

The difference is also one of perception. People who take LSD know they are on a drug and not experiencing reality. People who have NDEs perceive them as being vivid, intensely real experiences.

Morphine and Heroin: The hallucinations experienced from morphine and heroin are nothing like NDEs.

The hallucinations are rarely perceived as being real, but are usually recognized as narcotically induced.

More important, volunteers who have taken these narcotics describe nausea, vomiting, drowsiness, inability to concentrate, and even decreased vision.

For many, narcotics are a blissful and heavenly experience. But it does not involve traveling up a tunnel, seeing the Light, or having concrete visions of spirits, heaven, and God.

As a physician who paid his dues in Seattle's tough Harborview Hospital Emergency Room, I can confidently state that overdoses of narcotics do not create hallucinations that resemble NDEs. Here is one doctor's record of a test subject being given heroin:

"Fifteen minutes after injection, the subject began to laugh uncontrollably. He stated: 'I was seized by laughter and funny thoughts. Time sense for reading and counting was lost. Thoughts came in waves. I was saying things I didn't want to do or ought not to do.

(He made sexual advances on another subject.) I talked and talked and talked. I had some coffee and felt that I could kill someone. I felt I must have a psychiatric disorder, that this was my real true personality, which was evil, and coming out. I felt that I had no soul. (Monitors of the experiment) assured me that it was only the drug that I was taking. I wept.' ''

It is possible to pick out elements of this experience that are similar to NDEs, just as it is possible to pick out notes that children play on a piano that are used in Mozart's work. But on the whole, the two experiences can't compare.

"Recreational" Drugs: Research clearly shows that such drugs as marijuana, cocaine, PCP, amphetamines, and barbiturates do not cause NDE-like experiences.

In studies conducted at Stanford University, a great deal of paranoia was aroused in people who smoked high doses of both hashish and marijuana. One researcher reported that "Disorientation, speech disturbances, loss of control of thoughts, poor memory, depression, and outright fear were common."

A case study presented in the *Journal of the American Medical Association* of marijuana psychosis that occurred to a soldier in Vietnam offers an extreme example of drug paranoia at its worst:

"A 19-year-old, single, white soldier, private first class was referred for examination by another psychiatrist. He was alleged to have shot and killed an individual while on guard duty.

"Sworn statements and formal judicial investigation revealed that while on guard duty the victim shared a 'marihuana cigarette' with the subject, the subject's first. The victim was described as a joker whose humor was sometimes 'a little sick and cruel.' Shortly after having the cigarette the victim began to pick on some nearby Vietnamese children. He reportedly told them that he was 'Ho Chi Minh' and fired his weapon near them. Although the subject questioned if he was Ho Chi Minh, when the victim showed him the name on his shirt, the subject became terrified and fired his rifle. He then left his guard post and entered the base camp in a confused fashion, saying that he had killed Ho Chi Minh. Upon saying this he displayed a T-shirt with that name written on it and urged those around him to accompany him to see the body. On the way, he spoke in a disjointed and confused fashion. Upon arrival at the guard post, actually an observation tower, the bare-chested body of a Negro soldier, with several gunshot wounds on the left anterior portion of the chest, was found. . . . Upon examination the patient was confused and apprehensive, but quite proud of having killed Ho Chi Minh.

"The psychiatrist's opinion was that the subject was delusional and suffering from an acute toxic psychosis."

Although I admit that this is an extreme example of a drug-induced psychosis, it illustrates the paranoia that is frequently seen with drug usage and, in my experience, never seen in patients who have near-death experiences.

* * *

Anesthetic Agents: The most commonly used anesthetic agents, such as halothane, surital, nitrous oxide, narcotics, and Nembutal, simply do not cause hallucinations.

Following any surgical procedure, the patient may remember events and conversations heard during surgery and may become confused. For example, while under anesthesia my wife overheard a nurse discussing the death of her cat and became convinced that they were actually talking about her.

For this reason, such medications as Valium are given to create an amnesia for the time of the operation. Mystical hallucinations are simply not described in large studies of what patients recall while under anesthetic. Often patients remember music being played in the operating room, brief snatches of conversations, and the moods and emotions of the surgeon.

Ketamine: An anesthetic agent, Ketamine is no longer used because of its adverse psychological effects. Patients treated with Ketamine would frequently report frightening out-of-body episodes, not the pleasurable ones reported during NDEs. Also, their out-of-body experiences were of the autoscopic variety in which they saw mirror images of themselves and not the type experienced during an NDE in which a person hovers above an operating table, watching the action around him.

The following is an account of a patient who underwent minor surgery with Ketamine: "My mind left my body and apparently went to what some describe as a second state. I felt I was in a huge well-lit room, in front of a massive throne draped in lush velvet. I saw nothing else, but felt the presence of higher intelligences tapping my mind of every experience and impression I had gathered. I begged to be released, to return to my own body. It was terrifying.''

Ketamine hallucinations differ greatly from NDEs. There is a fearful and paranoid flavor not seen in NDEs. Also, patients know they are on drugs, and as a result, the experience does not seem real.

Transient Depersonalization: This theory states that patients who have near-fatal experiences become emotionally detached from their bodies. For them, life loses its meaning and intensity. There is a loss of emotion and time, and their own thought processes seem strange and unreal.

Swiss mountain-climbing journals contain excellent descriptions of depersonalization by climbers who fell from great heights but survived. Time slowed down for these climbers, and the entire experience seemed unreal as though the person were detached from the event.

This response allows a life-threatened person to handle a situation without panic and could permit him or her to initiate lifesaving measures.

Dr. Russel Noyes of the University of Iowa is the main proponent of the theory that NDEs are transient depersonalizations. However, in my research with children, I have not found them to report any of the aspects of depersonalization.

Memories of Birth: Carl Sagan, the Cornell University astronomer, explains near-death experiences as memory that is leftover from the experience of birth.

In his best-selling book, *Broca's Brain*, Sagan writes:

> The only alternative, so far as I can see, is that every human being, without exception, has already shared an experience like that of those travelers who return from the land of death: the sensation of flight; the emergence from darkness into light; an experience in which, at least sometimes, a heroic figure can be dimly perceived, bathed in radiance and glory. There is only one common experience that matches this description. It is called birth.

The theory that NDEs are memories of the birth experience has been challenged by many researchers, most notably Carl Becker, a philosophy professor from Southern Illinois University. Using existing research into infant perception and how much of the experience can actually be retained, he concludes that children have neither the eyesight nor the mental capacity to know or remember what is occurring during the birth process.

I have to wonder if the birth process, if it could be remembered at all, would be recalled in such a positive context. When one is pulled from a warm, supportive environment, and then cut with scissors to sever the umbilical cord, it is not a pleasant event to remember.

Also, the tunnel experience in an NDE involves rapid passage toward a light. In the birth experience, the child's face is pressed against the walls of the birth canal. The child can't see anything as he approaches life outside the womb.

Autoscopic Hallucinations: Autoscopy is the psychological event of seeing one's double. Although most people have never heard of it, it occurs in about two percent of the population.

This is actually seeing a mirror image of oneself. The image is dressed the same, and its movements usually mimic the person's own movements.

The double is often superimposed on reality. So if it walks in front of a window, the beholder cannot see out that window.

Autoscopy is usually associated with brain tumors, strokes, and migraine headaches. In fact, President Abraham Lincoln reported seeing his double hovering above him as he lay on a couch recovering from one of his frequent migraine headaches.

Some skeptics mistake out-of-body experiences for autoscopy. There is a great difference, however. In an out-of-body experience, a person sees himself from outside of his own body and from a perspective that is usually above. And he is seeing reality. The double is a hallucination projected upon reality.

Jung's *Collected Papers on Analytical Psychology* contains a report of a woman who had an autoscopic hallucination while having a splinter removed from her finger.

> Without any kind of bodily change she suddenly saw herself sitting by the side of a brook in a beautiful meadow, plucking flowers. This condition lasted as long as the slight operation and then disappeared spontaneously.

This experience differs greatly from an out-of-body experience in that the subject saw a facsimile of herself. In an out-of-body experience, the subject is actually outside his body watching activities that are going on in the room. For instance, here's an intriguing one from Dr. Raymond Moody's work:

> "As a resident, I was working in the emergency room when an elderly woman was brought in who was unconscious from a heart attack. I was giving her closed heart massage on an emergency room examining table and the nurse assisting me ran into another room to get a vial of medication that we needed.
> "It was a glass-necked vial that you're supposed to hold in a paper towel while breaking off the top so you don't cut yourself. When the nurse returned, the neck was broken so I could use the medicine right away.
> "When the old woman came to, she looked very sweetly at the nurse and said, 'Honey, I saw what you did in that room, and you're going to cut yourself doing that.' The nurse was shocked. She admitted that in her haste to open the medicine, she had broken the glass neck with her bare fingers.

"The woman told us that while we were resuscitating her, she had followed the nurse back to the room to watch what she was doing."

As you can see, an autoscopic hallucination and an out-of-body experience associated with an NDE are quite different.

The Endorphin Model: Endorphins are morphinelike chemicals produced in the brain to alleviate pain. They are responsible for such events as "the runner's high," that pleasurable feeling one has after exercise.

Endorphins were first related to NDEs by Dr. Daniel Carr of Massachusetts General Hospital. He states: "Within our brains is a neurotransmitter which acts similarly to morphine or heroin. This is a natural chemical, made by the brain, to respond to times of great pain. This is a natural high that is created by exercise, or creative energies, or religious faith. Any severe stress will create these natural 'endorphins' and they have many complex functions which can be summarized as reducing stress in the brain. No one has actually measured these endorphins or presented any sort of evidence at all that they are actually the chemicals created by the agonies of death, still, it is certainly reasonable to assume that the stresses of dying produce a lot of endorphins."

The Carr model is based on three points:

1. The brain, after being subjected to the sudden and unexperienced stress of dying, has the time to actually create a "large dose" of these mor-

phinelike chemicals. In many of the instances cited in this book, the brain would have to produce these chemicals within two or three minutes.

2. Morphinelike chemicals can actually generate near-death experiences.

3. The limbic lobe syndrome caused by these brain-produced chemicals is similar to NDEs.

There is no evidence in the medical literature that the stresses of dying actually produce significantly greater amounts of endorphins in the brain. In studies of animals dying of bacteria on the brain, small amounts of these chemicals are documented, yet their significance is unclear.

Most animal studies indicate that the brain becomes depleted of these endorphins, which makes sense since their main function is to alleviate pain and therefore would be depleted quickly. No evidence exists to prove that the dying brain makes large quantities of these chemicals.

Even Dr. Carr qualifies his theory by stating that there is no reason to suppose that endorphins are the main neurotransmitters involved in NDEs. He merely uses them as an example of a possible neurotransmitter.

Hypoxia: Simply stated, hypoxia is a lack of oxygen to the brain. In itself, it can certainly cause death, but does lack of oxygen necessarily cause death?

In our studies, we carefully examined medical records to see if there was a lack of oxygen in the blood gases. None of the patients who experienced NDEs was any more deprived of oxygen than the control groups that did not have NDEs.

In light of hypoxia, it is interesting to note the work of Dr. L. J. Medune, a professor of psychiatry at the University of Illinois School of Medicine in the 1940s and 1950s. Medune's theory was that mental illness represented a biochemical dysfunction within the brain and that treatments should be aimed at correcting that dysfunction. To do that, he had patients inhale high concentrations of carbon dioxide for a period of several minutes. Called ''the Medune mixture,'' its namesake predicted that general practitioners would be able to cure neurotics in their offices after a single, half-hour treatment. This would greatly benefit the poor, he declared, because they could easily afford this bottled psychiatric treatment as opposed to long-term psychotherapy.

The use of the Medune mixture was stopped in the sixties.

It is my hypothesis that such a high concentration of carbon dioxide caused the brain to trigger an NDE.

The Medune mixture certainly had the transformative effect of NDEs on its patients. And many of their descriptions of what happened while breathing the gas are in keeping with the stories told by NDEers.

TARGET OF REDUCTIONISM

After reading the data on these drug experiences and physiologic states, you might wonder why they are mistaken for NDEs. It is my feeling that near-death studies have become the target of reductionism because many researchers are frustrated at not being able to explain this spiritual phenomenon.

So for instance, a hallucination researcher such as Dr. Ronald Siegel studies the effects of drugs on the human mind and breaks down the hallucinations into very basic elements in an effort to understand the basic vocabulary of human hallucination.

He can point to drugs that cause tunnel experiences in some patients, or another drug that creates a variety of hallucinatory images, one of which is a bright star, and so on.

But near-death experiences appear to be a cluster of events so that one cannot understand the total by looking at its various pieces. One cannot understand music by studying the various frequencies of sound that generate each note, nor does one need to have a deep understanding of acoustical physics to enjoy Mozart. The near-death experience remains a mystery.

BIBLIOGRAPHY

The Age of the God-Kings: Ancient Egypt 3500–1500 B.C. New York: Time-Life Books, 1988.

Ariès, Philippe. *The Hour of Our Death*, trans. Helen Weaver. New York: Alfred A. Knopf, 1981.

———. *Western Attitudes Towards Death: From the Middle Ages to Present.* Baltimore, Md.: Johns Hopkins University Press, 1974.

Armstrong, Thomas. *The Radiant Child.* Wheaton, Ill.: Quest Books, 1985.

Bluebond-Langner, Myra. *The Private Worlds of Dying Children.* Princeton, N.J.: Princeton University Press, 1978.

Brim, Freeman, Levine, and Scotch, eds. *The Dying Patient.* New York: Russell Sage Foundation, 1970.

Brunton, A. P. *A Search in Secret Egypt.* New York: Samuel Weiser, 1984.

Budge, E. A. Wallis. *The Egyptian Book of the Dead.* New York: Dover Publications, 1967.

Campbell, Joseph. *Mythologies of the Primitive Hunters and Gatherers.* New York: Harper and Row, 1988.

———. *Myths to Live By.* New York: Bantam Books, 1972.

———. *The Masks of God: Primitive Mythology.* New York: Penguin Books, 1976.

———. *The Power of Myth.* New York: Doubleday, 1988.

———, ed. *The Mysteries: Papers from the Eranos Yearbooks.* Princeton, N.J.: Princeton University Press, Bollingen Series #30, 1955.

Changeux, Jean-Pierre. *Neuronal Man: The Biology of Mind.* New York: Oxford University Press, 1985.

Cook, Sarah Sheets. *Children and Dying: An Exploration and Selective Bibliographies.* New York: Health Sciences Publishing Corp., 1974.

Cranston, Sylvia, and Carey Williams. *Reincarnations: A New Ho-*

rizon in Science, Religion and Society. New York: Julian Press, 1984.

Ducasse, C. J. *The Belief in Life After Death*. Springfield, Ill.: Charles C. Thomas, 1961.

———. *Nature, Mind and Death*. Peru, Ill.: Open Court Publishing, 1951.

Edwards, Jonathan. "A Divine and Supernatural Light" and "Personal Narrative," in *The American Tradition in Literature*, edited by Bradley, Beatty, Long, and Perkins. New York: Grosset and Dunlap, 1956.

Evans-Wentz, W. Y. *The Tibetan Book of the Dead*. New York: Oxford University Press, 1960.

Feifel, Herman. *New Meanings of Death*. New York: McGraw-Hill, 1977.

Forti, Kathleen. *The Door to the Secret City*. Walpole, N.H.: Stillpoint Publishing, 1984.

Franz, Marie-Louise von. *Creation Myths*. Zurich: Spring Publications, 1978.

———. *On Dreams and Death*. Boston: Shambhala, 1987.

Frazer, James. *The Golden Bough*, abridged by Theodur Gaster. New York: New American Library. 1959.

Gabbard, Glen, and Stuart Twemlow. *With the Eyes of the Mind: An Empiric Analysis of Out-of-Body States*. New York: Praeger, 1984.

Gardner, Howard. *The Mind's New Science: A History of the Cognitive Revolution*. New York: Basic Books, 1987.

Gimbutas, Marija. *The Goddesses and Gods of Old Europe: Myths and Cult Images*. Los Angeles and Berkeley: University of California Press, 1982.

Griffiths, J. G. *Apuleius of Madura: The Isis Book*. Leiden, The Netherlands: E. J. Brill, 1975.

Grof, Stanislav and Christina. *Beyond Death*. New York: Thames & Hudson, 1980.

Grof, Stanislav, and Joan Halifax. *The Human Encounter with Death*. New York: E. P. Dutton, 1977.

Haggard, Howard. *Devils, Drugs and Doctors: The Science of Healing from Medicine Man to Doctor*. New York: Harper and Row, 1929.

Hooper, Judith, and Dick Teresi. *The Three Pound Universe: The Brain, From the Chemistry of the Mind to the Frontiers of the Soul*. New York: Dell Books, 1986.

I Never Saw Another Butterfly: Children's Drawings and Poems from Terezin Concentration Camp. New York: Schocken Books, 1978.

James, William. *The Varieties of Religious Experience: A Study in Human Nature*. New York: The Modern Library, 1936.

Jaynes, Julian. *The Origin of Consciousness in the Breakdown of the Bicameral Mind*. Boston: Houghton Mifflin, 1976.

Jung, C. G. *Modern Man in Search of a Soul*. New York: Harcourt, Brace and World, 1933.

Kastenbaum, Robert. *Between Life and Death*. New York: Springer Publishing, 1979.

———. *Is There Life After Death?* Englewood Cliffs, N.J.: Prentice-Hall, 1984.

Kübler-Ross, Elisabeth. *On Children and Death*. New York: Macmillan Publishing Co., 1983.

———. *On Death and Dying*. New York: Macmillan Publishing Co., 1969.

Kuhn, Thomas. *The Structure of Scientific Revolution*. Chicago: University of Chicago Press, 1970.

Kutscher, Austin. *Death and Bereavement*. Springfield, Ill.: Charles C. Thomas, 1969.

Lauf, Detlef Ingo. *Secret Doctrines of the Tibetan Books of the Dead*. Boulder, Colo.: Shambhala Publishing, 1977.

Levine, Stephen. *Meetings at the Edge: Dialogues with the Grieving and the Dying, the Healing and the Healed*. New York: Doubleday and Company, 1984.

Lindsay, Jack. *The Origins of Alchemy in Graeco-Roman Egypt*. London: Frederick Muller, 1970.

Maslow, A. H. *The Farther Reaches of Human Nature*. New York: Viking Press, Esalon Books, 1971.

Mishlove, Jeffrey. *The Roots of Consciousness*. New York: Random House, 1975.

Medune, L. J. *Carbon Dioxide Therapy: A Neurophysiological Treatment of Nervous Disorders*. Springfield, Ill.: Charles C. Thomas, 1950.

Moody, Raymond. *The Light Beyond*. New York: Bantam Books, 1988.

———. *Life after Life*. 1975.

———. *Reflections on Life after Life*. New York: Bantam Books, 1977.

Neihardt, John G. *Black Elk Speaks*. Lincoln: University of Nebraska Press, 1932.

Ornstein, Robert. *The Psychology of Consciousness*. New York: Penguin Books, 1977.

Osis, Karlis. *Deathbed Observations by Physicians and Nurses*. Parapsychological Monographs, Number 3. New York: Parapsychological Foundation, Inc., 1961.

Penfield, Wilder. *The Mystery of the Mind: A Critical Study of Consciousness and the Human Brain*. Princeton, N.J.: Princeton University Press, 1975.

—— and Theodore Rasmussen. *The Cerebral Cortex of Man*. New York: Macmillan Publishing Co., 1950.

Plato. *The Republic*, trans. Francis Cornford. New York: Oxford University Press, 1941.

Plum, Fred, and Jerome Posner. *The Diagnosis of Stupor and Coma*. Philadelphia: F. A. Davis Company, 1977.

Provonsha, Jack. *Is Death for Real: An Examination of Reported Near-Death Experiences in the Light of the Resurrection*. Boise, Idaho: Pacific Press, 1981.

Psychic Voyages. New York: Time-Life Books, 1988.

Reiff, Robert, and Martin Scheerer. *Memory and Hypnotic Age Regression*. New York: International Universities Press, 1959.

Restak, Richard. *The Brain*. New York: Bantam Books, 1984.

——. *The Mind*. New York: Bantam Books, 1988.

Ring, Kenneth. *Heading toward Omega: In Search of the Meaning of the Near-Death Experience*. New York: William Morrow, 1984.

——. *Life at Death: A Scientific Investigation of the Near-Death Experience*. New York: Quill, 1982.

Rorty, Richard. *Philosophy and the Mirror of Nature*. Princeton, N.J.: Princeton University Press, 1979.

Sabom, Michael. *Recollections of Death: A Medical Investigation*. New York: Harper and Row, 1982.

Sanders, N. K. *The Epic of Gilgamesh*. New York: Penguin Books, 1960.

Schure, E. *The Mysteries of Ancient Egypt*. Blauvelt, N.Y.: Rudolf Steiner Publications, 1971.

Seifert, W. *Neurobiology of the Hippocampus*. New York: Academic Press, 1983.

Sorensen, Michelle. *The Journey Beyond Life*. Orem, Utah: Family Affair, 1988.

Taylor, Gordon. *The Natural History of the Mind*. New York: Penguin Books, 1986.

Taylor, T. *The Eleusinian and Bacchic Mysteries*. San Diego, Calif.: Wizards Bookshelf, 1980.

Temple, Robert. *The Sirius Mystery*. New York: St. Martin's Press, 1976.

Thompson, C.J.S. *The Hand of Destiny: The Folklore and Superstitions of Everyday Life*. Detroit, Mich.: Singing Tree Press, 1970.

——. *The Mystery and Lore of Apparitions: With Some Account of Ghosts, Spectres, Phantoms and Boggarts in Early Times*. New York: Frederick Stokes, 1931.

Thomson, William. *The Brain and Personality: or the Physical Relations of the Brain to the Mind*. New York: Dodd, Mead and Company, 1919.

Winson, Jonathan. *Brain and Psyche: The Biology of the Unconscious*. New York: Vintage Books, 1986.

Wixon, Hartt and Judene. *Trial by Terror: The Child-Hostage Crisis in Cokeville, Wyoming*. Bountiful, Utah: Horizon Publishers, 1987.

Young, J. Z. *Philosophy and the Brain*. New York: Oxford University Press, 1988.

Yzcorzynski, G. K.; A. J. Atkinson; J. Cohen; and F. G. Shufflebarger. *Investigation of Carbon Dioxide Therapy*. Springfield, Ill.: Charles C. Thomas, 1962.

Zaleski, Carol. *Otherworld Journeys: Accounts of Near-Death Experience in Medieval and Modern Times*. New York: Oxford University Press, 1987.

SELECTED BIBLIOGRAPHY OF PAPERS REFERRED TO IN TEXT

Ayers Counts, Dorothy. "Near-Death Experiences and Out-of-Body Experiences in a Melanesian Society. *Anabiosis* 3 (1983):115–36.

Babb, T. L., C. L. Wilson, and I. Isokawa-Akesson. "Firing Patterns of Human Limbic Neurons During Stereoencephalography and Clinical Temporal Lobe Seizures." *Electroencephalography and Clinical Neurophysiology* 66(1987): 467–82.

Bauer, Martin. "Near-Death Experiences and Attitude Change." *Anabiosis* 5(1985): 39–47.

Baxter, S. "Psychological Problems of Intensive Care." *Br J Hosp Med* 41(1974): 875–85.

Becker, C. B. "Views from Tibet: NDEs and the Book of the Dead." *Anabiosis* 5(1985): 3–20.

Blacher, R. S. "Awareness During Surgery." *Anesthesiology* 61(1984): 1–2.

Blachy, P. H., Starr, A. "Post-Cardiotomy Delirium." *Am J Psych* 121(4) (1964): 371–74.

Burche, G. E., N. P. Depasquale, and J. H. Phillips. "What Is Death." *Am Heart J* (September 1968): 438–39.

Cahal, D. A. "Effects of Nalorphine on the Behavior of Healthy Human Volunteers." *J Ment Sci* 103(1957): 850–55.

Carr, D. "Pathophysiology of Stress-Induced Limbic Lobe Dysfunction: A Hypothesis for NDEs." *Anabiosis* 2(1982): 75–90.

Collier, B.: "Ketamine and the Conscious Mind." *Anesthesiology* 27(1972): 120–34.

Collier, B. "Ketamine and the Near-Death Experience." *Anabiosis* 1(1984): 87–96.

Comer, N. L., L. Madow, and J. Dixon. "Observations of Sensory Deprivation in a Life-Threatening Situation." *Am J Psych* 124(1967): 164–67.

Dingledine, R., M. A. Hynes, and G. L. King. "Involvement of

N-Methyl-D-Aspartate Receptors in Epileptiform Bursting in the Rat Hippocampal Slice.'' *Journal of Physiology* 380(1986): 175–89.

Domino, E. F., and P. Chodoff. "Corssen: Human Pharmacology of CI-581, a New Intravenous Agent Chemically Related to Phencyclidine." *Federal Proceedings* 24(1965): 268.

Ehrenwald, J. "Out-of-Body Experiences and the Denial of Death." *J Nerv Men Dis* 159(1974): 227–33.

Engel, G. L. "The Need for a New Medical Model: A Challenge for Biomedicine." *Science 196* (April 8, 1977): 129–35.

Ferguson, S. M., Rayport, M., Gardner, R., et al. "Similarities in Mental Content of Psychotic States, Spontaneous Seizures, Dreams, and Responses to Electrical Brain Stimulation in Patients with Temporal Lobe Epilepsy." *Psychosom Med* 31(1969): 479–98.

Fujiwara, N., et al. "Effects of Hypoxia on Rat Hippocampal Neurons in Vitro." 384(1987): 131–51.

Gabbard, Glen, and Stuart Twemlow. "An Overview of Altered Mind/Body Perception." *Bulletin of the Menninger Clinic* 50 (July 1986): 351–66.

Gabbard, Glen, Stuart Twemlow, and F. C. Jones. "Do Near-Death Experiences Only Occur Near Death." *J Nerv Men Dis* 169(1981): 374–77.

Gardner, G. G. "Childhood, Death and Human Dignity: Hypnotherapy for David." *The International Journal of Clinical and Experimental Hypnosis* 24(1976): 122–39.

Green, J. T., and P. Friedman. "Near-Death Experiences in a Southern California Population." *Anabiosis* 3(1983): 77–96.

Greyson, Bruce. "The Psychodynamics of the Near-Death Experience." *J Nerv Men Dis* 6(1983): 376–81.

——. "A Typology of Near-Death Experiences." *Am J Psych* 142(August 1985): 967–69.

—— and I. Stevenson. "The Phenomenology of Near-Death Experiences." *Am J Psych* 137(1980): 1193–96.

Grosso, Michael. "NDEs and Archetypes." *Anabiosis* 4(Fall 1984): 178–79.

——. "Self: Eternity, and the Mysteries: A Speculative Response to Kenneth Ring's Paper." *Anabiosis* 4(1984): 153–62.

Heim, A. "Notizen ueber den Tod durch Absturz." *Jahrbuch Schweiz. Alpen Klub* 27(1882): 327.

Herzog, D. B., and J. T. Herrin. "Near-Death Experiences in the Very Young." *Critical Care Medicine* 13(1985): 1074–75.

Hollister, L. E. "Drug-Induced Psychoses and Schizophrenic Reactions: A Critical Comparison." *Ann NY Acad Sci* 96(1962): 80–93.

Jacobs, T. J., and E. Charles. "Life Events and the Occurrence of Cancer in Children." *Psychosomatic Medicine* 42(1980): 11–24.

Judson, I. R., and E. Wiltshaw. "A Near-Death Experience." *Lancet* 2(1983): 561–62.

Kanigel, Robert. "Placebos, Magic Medicine?" *Johns Hopkins Magazine* (August 1983): 12–16.

Katz, N. M., D. P. Agle, and R. G. DePalma, et al. "Delirium in Surgical Patients Under Intensive Care." *Arch Surg* 104(1972): 310–13.

Kirshnan, V. "Near-Death Experiences: Evidence for Survival?" *Anabiosis* 5(Spring 1986): 21–38.

Lisandky, J., Strassman, R. J., Janowsky, D., et al. "Drug-Induced Psychosis," in Tupin, J. P., Halbreich, U., Pena, J. J. (eds.): *Transient Psychosis: Diagnosis, Management and Evaluation.* New York: Brunner/Mazel, Inc., 1984.

Lundahl, C. R., and H. A. Widdison. "The Mormon Explanation of Near-Death Experiences." *Anabiosis* 3(1983): 97–106.

M-Marsel, Mesulam. "Dissociative States with Abnormal Temporal Lobe EEG: Multiple Personalities and the Illusion of Possession." *Arch Neurol* 38(March 1981): 176–81.

Milner, B. "Further Analysis of the Hippocampal Amnesiac Syndrome: Fourteen-Year Follow-Up Study of H.M." *Neuropsychologia* (1968): 215–34.

Morse, M., P. Castillo, D. Venecia, et al. "Childhood Near-Death Experiences." *ADJC* 140(1986): 1110–1113.

Morse, M. L., D. Connor, and D. Tyler. "Near-Death Experiences in a Pediatric Population." *ADJC* 139(1985): 595–600.

Noyes, R. "Near-Death Experiences: Their Interpretation and Significance," in Kastenbaum, R. (ed.): *Between Life and Death.* New York: Springer, 1979.

Papez, J. W. "A Proposed Mechanism of Emotion." *Archives of Neurology and Psychiatry* (1937): 725–43.

Pardes, H. "Neuroscience and Psychiatry: Marriage or Coexistence?" *Am J Psych* 143(1986): 1205–12.

Pasricha, Satwant, and Ian Stevenson. "Near-Death Experiences in India: A Preliminary Report." *J Nerv Men Dis* 175(March 1986): 65–170.

Penfield, W. "The Role of the Temporal Cortex in Certain Psychical Phenomena." *J Ment Sci* 101(1955): 451–65.

Raft, David, and Jeffry Andersen. "Transformations in Self-Understanding After Near-Death Experiences." *Contemporary Psychoanalysis* 22(July 1986): 319–46.

Ring, Kenneth. "From Alpha to Omega: Ancient Mysteries and the Near-Death Experience." *Anabiosis* 5(1987): 3–16.

Rodabough, Tillman. "Near-Death Experiences: An Examination of the Supporting Data and Alternative Explanations." *Death Studies* 9(1985): 95–113.

Rogo, D. S. "Ketamine and the Near-Death Experience." *Anabiosis* 1(1984): 87–96.

———. "NDEs and Archetypes: Reply." *Anabiosis* 4(Fall 1984): 180.

Rothman, S. M., J. H. Thurston, G. D. Clark, et al. "Ketamine Protects Hippocampal Neurons from Anoxia in Vitro. *Neuroscience* 21(1987): 673–78.

Saavedra-Aguilar, J. C., and J. S. Gomez-Jeria. "A Neurobiological Model for Near-Death Experiences." *Journal of Near-Death Studies* (in press).

Schenk, L., and D. Bear. "Multiple Personality and Related Dissociative Phenomena in Patients with Temporal Lobe Epilepsy." *Am J Psych* 138(October 1981): 1311–15.

Schnapper, N. "The Psychological Implications of Severe Trauma: Emotional Sequelae to Unconsciousness." *J Trauma* 15(1975): 94–98.

Serdahely, W. J. "A Pediatric Near-Death Experience: Tunnel Variants." *Omega* 20(1989–90): 55–62.

Siegel, Ronald. "The Psychology of Life After Death." *American Psychologist* 35(October 1980): 911–31.

Siegel, Ronald, and Ada Hirschman. "Hashish Near-Death Experiences." *Anabiosis* 4(Spring 1984): 69–86.

Snow, A., S. Tucker, and W. Dewey. "The Role of Neurotransmitters in Stress-Induced Antinociception." *Pharm Biochem Behav* 16(1982): 47–50.

Staib, A. R., and D. R. Logan. "Hypnotic Stimulation of Breast Growth." *Am J Clin Hypn* 19(1977): 201.

Stephens, J. H., J. W. Shaffer, and W. T. Carpenter. "Reactive Psychoses." *J Nerv Ment Dis* 170(1982): 657–66.

Strahlendorf, F., G. Goldstein, G. Rossi, et al. "Differential Effects of LSD, Serotonin, and L-Tryptophan on Visually Evoked Responses." *Pharm Biochem Behav* 16(1982): 51–55.

White, F., and T. Appel. "Lysergic Acid Diethylamide and Lisuride: Differentiation of Their Neuropharmacological Actions." *Science* 216(1982): 535–36.

Talbott, J. A., J. W. Teague. "Marijuana psychosis." *JAMA* 210(1969): 299–302.

Wiener, J. M. "Response of Medical and Paramedical Personnel to Fatal Illness and Death of a Child in Loss and Grief: Psychological Management in Medical Practice.''

Willard, R. D. ''Breast Enlargement Through Visual Imagery and Hypnosis.'' *Am J Clin Hypn* 19(1977): 195.

Williams, J. E. ''Stimulation of Breast Growth by Hypnosis.'' *Journal of Sex Research* 10(1974): 316.

Wilson, S. L., R. W. Vaughan, and C. R. Stephen. ''Awareness, Dreams, and Hallucinations Associated with General Anesthesia.'' *Anesth Analg* 5(1975): 609–17.

Winson, J., and C. Abzug. ''Gating of Neuronal Transmission in the Hippocampus.'' *Science* 196(1977): 1223.

——. ''Neuronal Transmission Through Hippocampal Pathways Dependent on Behavior.'' *Journal of Neurophysiology* 41(1978): 716–22.

Wooston, J. L. ''Psychiatric Aspects of a Pediatric Intensive Care Unit.'' *Yale J Biol Med* 57(1984): 97–110.

About the Authors

MELVIN MORSE, M.D., is a graduate of George Washington University School of Medicine and a recipient of the National Service Research Award. He is a recognized authority in the field of near-death studies and has researched near-death experiences in children for eight years.

Dr. Morse has a busy private practice in the suburbs of Seattle, Washington, where he lives with his wife and their three children.

PAUL PERRY is former executive editor of *American Health Magazine* and a Gannett Center for Media Studies scholar. He has coauthored two books with Dr. Raymond Moody, the acknowledged father of near-death studies.

He lives in Scottsdale, Arizona, with his wife and three children.